MISCELLANEOUS STUDIES
IN PROSE

PRACTICAL ENGLISH SERIES

MISCELLANEOUS STUDIES IN PROSE

COMPILED BY
GRENVILLE KLEISER

*For the Exclusive Use of Grenville Kleiser's
Mail Course Students*

FUNK & WAGNALLS COMPANY
NEW YORK AND LONDON

COPYRIGHT, 1911, BY
GRENVILLE KLEISER
Printed in the United States of America

TO THE STUDENT

It is generally recognized that clear and accurate thinking must precede clear and accurate expression. The selections presented here have a double value for the student. First, as examples of clear and forceful thinking; second, as specimens of good English.

The student of English should be a general reader of the recognized stylists. These extracts should stimulate his interest in the larger works of such writers as Addison, Carlyle, Macaulay and Newman. Webster should be closely studied as a master of English style, with special regard to the needs of the public speaker.

The chapter entitled "Speech and Thought," from Lotze's famous work, "Microcosmus," is particularly commended to the student's attention, and is reprinted here by special permission of the publishers.

GRENVILLE KLEISER.

CONTENTS

SIR ROGER DE COVERLEY
  By Joseph Addison (1672-1719) . 1
DARTMOUTH COLLEGE CASE
  By Daniel Webster (1782-1852) . 6
WILLIAM PITT
  By Thomas Carlyle (1795-1881) . 71
ON THE ATHENIAN ORATORS
  By Thomas Babington Macaulay (1800-1859) 90
LITERATURE
  By John Henry Newman (1801-1890) 112
SPEECH AND THOUGHT
  By Rudolf Hermann Lotze (1817-1881) 139

Miscellaneous Studies in Prose

SIR ROGER DE COVERLEY

BY JOSEPH ADDISON

The first and most obvious reflections which arise in a man who changes the city for the country are upon the different manners of the people whom he meets with in those two different scenes of life. By manners I do not mean morals, but behavior and good-breeding as they show themselves in the town and in the country.

And here, in the first place, I must observe a very great revolution that has happened in this article of good-breeding. Several obliging deferences, condescensions, and submissions, with many outward forms and ceremonies that accompany them, were first of all brought up among the politer part of mankind, who lived in courts and cities, and distinguished themselves from the rustic part of the species (who on all occasions acted bluntly and naturally) by such a mutual complaisance and intercourse of civilities. These forms of conversation by degrees multiplied and grew troublesome; the modish world found too great a constraint in them, and have therefore thrown most of them aside. Conversation, like the Romish religion, was so encumbered with show and ceremony that it stood in need of a reformation to retrench its superfluities and restore it to its natural good sense and beauty. At present, therefore, an unconstrained carriage and a certain openness of behavior are the height of good-breeding. The fashionable world is grown free and easy; our manners sit more loose upon us. Nothing is so modish as an agreeable negligence. In a word, good-breeding shows itself most where to an ordinary eye it appears the least.

If after this we look on the people of mode in the country we find in them the manners of the last age. They have no sooner fetched themselves up to the fashion of the polite world but the town has dropt them, and are nearer to the first state of nature than to those refinements which formerly reigned in the court, and still prevail in the country. One may now know a man that never conversed in the world by his excess of good-breeding. A polite country squire shall make you as many bows in half an hour as would serve a courtier for a week. There is infinitely more to do about place and precedency in a meeting of justices' wives than in an assembly of duchesses.

This rural politeness is very troublesome to a man of my temper, who generally take the chair that is next me, and walk first or last, in the front or in the rear, as chance directs. I have known my friend Sir Roger's dinner almost cold before the company could adjust the ceremonial and be prevailed upon to sit down; and have heartily pitied my old friend, when I have seen him forced to pick and cull his guests, as they sat at the several parts of his table, that he might drink their healths according to their respective ranks and qualities. Honest Will Wimble, who I should have thought had been altogether uninfected with ceremony, gives me abundance of trouble in this particular. Tho he has been fishing all the morning, he will not help himself at dinner till I am served. When we are going out of the hall he runs behind me; and last night, as we were walking in the fields, stopt short at a stile till I came up to it, and upon my making signs to him to get over, told me, with a serious smile, that sure I believed they had no manners in the country.

There has happened another revolution in the point of good-breeding, which relates to the conversation among men of mode, and which I can not but look upon as very extraordinary. It was certainly one of the first distinctions of a well-bred man to express everything that had the most remote appearance of being obscene in modest terms and distant phrases; while the clown, who had no such delicacy of conception and expression, clothed his ideas in those plain, homely terms that are the most obvious and natural. This kind of good manners was perhaps carried to an excess, so as to make conversation too stiff, formal, and precise; for which reason (as hypocrisy in one age is generally succeeded by atheism in another) conversation is in a great measure relapsed into the first extreme; so that at present several of our men of the town, and particularly those who have been polished in France, make use of the most coarse, uncivilized words in our language, and utter themselves often in such a manner as a clown would blush to hear.

This infamous piece of good-breeding, which reigns among the coxcombs of the town, has not yet made its way into the country; and as it is impossible for such an irrational way of conversation to last long among a people that make any profession of religion, or show of modesty, if the country gentlemen get into it they will certainly be left in the lurch. Their good-breeding will come too late to them, and they will be thought a parcel of lewd clowns, while they fancy themselves talking together like men of wit and pleasure.

As the two points of good-breeding which I have hitherto insisted upon regard behavior and conversation, there is a third, which turns upon dress. In this, too, the country are very much behindhand. The rural beaus are not yet got out of the fashion that took place at the time of the Revolution, but ride about the country in red coats and laced hats, while the women in many parts are still trying to outvie one another in the height of their head-dresses.

But a friend of mine, who is now upon the western circuit, having promised to give me an account of the several modes and fashions that prevail in the different parts of the nation through which he passes, I shall defer the enlarging upon this last topic till I have received a letter from him, which I expect every post.

THE DARTMOUTH COLLEGE CASE*

BY DANIEL WEBSTER

(Argument before the Supreme Court of the United States, at Washington, on the 10th of March, 1818.)

(The action, The Trustees of Dartmouth College, vs. William H. Woodward, was commenced in the Court of Common Pleas, Grafton County, State of New Hampshire, February term, 1817. The declaration was trover for the books of record, original charter, common seal, and other corporate property of the college. The conversion was alleged to have been made on the 7th day of October, 1816. The proper pleas were filed, and by consent the cause was carried directly to the Supreme Court of New Hampshire, by appeal, and entered at the May term, 1817. The general issue was pleaded by the defendant, and joined by the plaintiffs. The facts in the case were then agreed upon by the parties, and drawn up in the form of a special verdict, reciting the charter of the college and the acts of the legislature of the State, passed June and December, 1816, by which the said corporation of Dartmouth College was *enlarged* and *improved*, and the said charter *amended*.

The question made in the case was, whether those acts of the legislature were valid and binding upon the corporation, without their acceptance or assent, and not repugnant to the Constitution of the United States. If so, the verdict found for the defendants; otherwise, it found for the plaintiffs.

The case was continued to the September term of the court in Rockingham County, where it was argued; and at the November term of the same year, in Grafton County, the opinion of the court was delivered by Chief Justice Richardson, in favor of

*Published by kind permission of Little, Brown & Company.

STUDIES IN PROSE

the validity and constitutionality of the acts of the legislature; and judgment was accordingly entered for the defendant on the special verdict.

Thereupon a writ of error was sued out by the original plaintiffs, to remove the cause to the Supreme Court of the United States; where it was entered at the term of the court held at Washington, on the first Monday of February, 1818.

The cause came on for argument on the 10th day of March, 1818, before all the judges. It was argued by Mr. Webster and Mr. Hopkinson for the plaintiffs in error, and by Mr. Holmes and the Attorney-General (Writ) for the defendant in error.

At the term of the court held in February, 1819, the opinion of the judges was delivered by Chief Justice Marshall, declaring the acts of the legislature unconstitutional and invalid, and reversing the judgment of the State Court. The Court, with the exception of Mr. Justice Duvall, were unanimous.

The following was the argument of Mr. Webster for the plaintiffs in error.)

THE general question is, whether the acts of the Legislature of New Hampshire of the 27th of June, and of the 18th and 26th of December, 1816, are valid and binding on the plaintiffs, *without their acceptance or assent.*

The charter of 1769 created and established a corporation, to consist of twelve persons, and no more; to be called the "Trustees of Dartmouth College." The preamble to the charter recites that it is granted on the application and request of the Rev. Eleazer Wheelock: That Doctor Wheelock, above the year 1754, established a charity school, at his own

7

expense, and on his own estate and plantation; That for several years, through the assistance of well-disposed persons in America, granted at his solicitation, he had clothed, maintained, and educated a number of native Indians, and employed them afterward as missionaries and schoolmasters among the savage tribes: That his design promising to be useful, he had constituted the Rev. Mr. Whitaker to be his attorney, with power to solicit contributions in England, for the further extension and carrying on of his undertaking; and that he had requested the Earl of Dartmouth, Baron Smith, Mr. Thornton, and other gentlemen to receive such sums as might be contributed in England toward supporting his school, and to be trustees thereof, for his charity; which these persons had agreed to do: That thereupon Doctor Wheelock had executed to them a deed of trust, in pursuance of such agreement between him and them, and, for divers good reasons, had referred it to these persons to determine the place in which the school should be finally established. And, to enable them to form a proper decision on this subject, had laid before them the several offers which had been made to him by the several governments in America, in order to induce him to settle and establish his school within the limits of such governments for their own emolument and the increase of learning in their respective places, as well as for the furtherance of his general original design: And inasmuch as a number of the proprietors of lands in New Hampshire, animated by the example of the Governor himself and others, and in consideration that, without any impediment to its original design, the school might be enlarged and improved, to promote learning among the English, and to supply ministers to the people of the Province, had promised large tracts of land, provided the school should be established in that Province, the persons before mentioned having weighed the reasons in favor of the several places proposed, had given the preference to this Province and these offers: That Doctor Wheelock therefore represented the necessity of a legal incorporation, and proposed that certain gentlemen in America whom he had already named and appointed in his will to be trustees of his charity after his decease, should compose the corporation. Upon this recital, and in consideration of the laudable original design of Doctor Wheelock, and willing that the best means of education be established in New Hampshire for the benefit of the Province, the king granted the charter, by the advice of his Provincial Council.

The substance of the facts thus recited is, that Doctor Wheelock has founded a charity on funds owned and procured by himself; that he was at that time the sole dispenser and sole administrator, as well as the legal owner, of these funds; that he had made his will, devising this property in trust, to continue the existence and uses of the school, and appointed trustees; that, in this state of things, he had been invited to fix his school permanently in New Hampshire, and to extend the design of it to the education of the youth of that Province; that before he removed his school, or accepted this invitation, which his friends in England had advised him to accept, he applied for a charter, to be granted, not to whomsoever the king or government of the Province should please, but to such persons as he named and appointed, namely, the persons whom he had already appointed to be the future trustees of his charity by his will.

The charter, or letters patent, then proceed to create such a corporation, and to appoint twelve persons to constitute it, by the name of the "Trustees of Dartmouth College"; to have perpetual existence as such corporation, and with power to hold and dispose of lands and goods, for the use of the college, with all the ordinary powers of corporations. They are in their discretion to apply the funds and property of the college to the support of the president, tutors, ministers, and other officers of the college, and such missionaries and schoolmasters as they may see fit to employ among the Indians. There are to be twelve trustees *forever, and no more,* and they are to have the right of filling vacancies occurring in their own body. The Rev. Mr. Wheelock

STUDIES IN PROSE

is declared to be the founder of the college, and is, by the charter, appointed first president, with power to appoint a successor by his last will. All proper powers of government, superintendence and visitation are vested in the trustees. They are to appoint and remove all officers at their discretion, to fix their salaries and assign their duties, and to make all ordinances, orders, and laws for the government of the students. To the end that the persons who had acted as depositaries of the contributions in England, and who had also been contributors themselves, might be satisfied of the good use of their contributions, the president was annually, or when required, to transmit to them an account of the progress of the institution and the disbursements of its funds, so long as they should continue to act in that trust. These letters patent are to be good and effectual, in law, *against the king, his heirs and successors forever,* without further grant or confirmation; and the trustees are to hold all and singular these privileges, advantages, liberties and immunities to them and to their successors forever.

No funds are given to the college by this charter. A corporate existence and capacity are given to the trustees, with the privileges and immunities mentioned, to enable the founder and his associates better to manage the funds they themselves had contributed, and such others as they might afterward obtain.

After the institution thus created and constituted had existed, uninterruptedly and usefully, nearly fifty years, the legislature of New Hampshire passed the acts in question.

The first makes the twelve trustees under the charter, and nine other individuals, to be appointed by the Governor and Council, a corporation, by a new name; and to this new corporation transfers all the *property, rights, powers, liberties, and privileges* of the old corporation; with further power to establish new colleges and an institute, and to apply all or any part of the funds to these purposes; subject to the power and control of a board of twenty-five overseers, to be appointed by the Governor and Council.

The second act makes further provisions for executing the objects of the first, and the last act authorizes the defendant, the treasurer of the plaintiffs, to retain and hold their property against their will.

If these acts are valid, the old corporation is abolished and a new one created. The first act does, in fact, if it can have any effect, create a new corporation, and transfer to it all the property and franchises of the old. The two corporations are not the same in anything which essentially belongs to the existence of a corporation. They have different names, and different powers, rights and duties. Their organization is wholly different. The powers of the corporation are not vested in the same or

STUDIES IN PROSE

similar hands. In one, the trustees are twelve and no more. In the other, they are twenty-one. In one the power is in a single board. In the other it is divided between two boards. Altho the act professes to include the old trustees in the new corporation, yet that was without their assent, and against their remonstrance; and no person can be compelled to be a member of such a corporation against his will. It was neither expected nor intended that they should be members of the new corporation. The act itself treats the old corporation as at an end, and, going on the ground that all its functions have ceased, it provides for the first meeting and organization of the new corporation. It expressly provides also that the new corporation shall have and hold all the property of the old, a provision which would be quite unnecessary upon any other ground than that the old corporation was dissolved. But if it could be contended that the effect of these acts was not entirely to abolish the old corporation, yet it is manifest that they impair and invade the rights, property, and powers of the trustees under the charter, as a corporation, and the legal rights, privileges and immunities which belong to them as individual members of the corporation.

The twelve trustees were the *sole* legal owners of all they acquired under the charter. By the acts others are admitted, against *their* will, to be joint owners. The twelve individuals who are trustees were possest of all the franchises and immunities conferred by the charter. By the acts *nine* other trustees and *twenty-five* overseers are admitted, against their will, to divide these franchises and immunities with them.

If, either as a corporation or as individuals, they have any legal rights, this forcible intrusion of others violates those rights, as manifestly as an entire and complete ouster and dispossession. These acts alter the whole constitution of the corporation. They affect the rights of the whole body as a corporation, and the rights of the individuals who compose it. They revoke corporate powers and franchises. They alienate and transfer the property of the college to others. By the charter the trustees had a right to fill vacancies in their own number. This was now taken away. They were to consist of twelve, and, by express provision, of no more. This is altered. They and their successors, appointed by themselves, were forever to hold the property. The legislature has found successors for them before their seats are vacant. The powers and privileges which the twelve were to exercise exclusively are now to be exercised by others. By one of the acts they are subjected to heavy penalties if they exercise their offices, or any of those powers and privileges granted them by charter, and which they had exercised for fifty years. They

STUDIES IN PROSE

are to be punished for not accepting the new grant and taking its benefits. This, it must be confest, is rather a summary mode of settling a question of constitutional rights. Not only are new trustees forced into the corporation, but new trusts and uses are created. The college is turned into a university. Power is given to create new colleges, and, to authorize any diversion of the funds which may be agreeable to the new boards, sufficient latitude is given by the undefined power of establishing an institute. To these new colleges and this institute the funds contributed by the founder, Doctor Wheelock, and by the original donors, the Earl of Dartmouth and others, are to be applied in plain and manifest disregard of the uses to which they were given.

The president, one of the old trustees, had a right to his office, salary, and emoluments, subject to the twelve trustees alone. His title to these is now changed and he is made accountable to new masters. So also all the professors and tutors. If the legislature can at pleasure make these alterations and changes in the rights and privileges of the plaintiffs, it may, with equal propriety, abolish these rights and privileges altogether. The same power which can do any part of this work can accomplish the whole. And, indeed, the argument on which these acts have been hitherto defended goes altogether to the ground, that this is such a corporation as the legislature may abolish at pleasure; and that its members have no rights, *liberties, franchises, property, or privileges,* which the legislature may not revoke, annul, alienate or transfer to others, whenever it sees fit.

It will be contended by the plaintiffs that these acts are not valid and binding on them without their assent:

1. Because they are against common right and the Constitution of New Hampshire.

2. Because they are repugnant to the Constitution of the United States.

I am aware of the limits which bound the jurisdiction of the court in this case, and that on this record nothing can be decided but the single question, whether these acts are repugnant to the Constitution of the United States. Yet it may assist in forming an opinion of their true nature and character to compare them with those fundamental principles introduced into the State governments for the purpose of limiting the exercise of the legislative power, and which the constitution of New Hampshire expresses with great fulness and accuracy.

It is not much to assert that the Legislature of New Hampshire would not have been competent to pass the acts in question, and to make them binding on the plaintiffs without their assent, even if there had been, in the Constitution of New Hampshire or of the United States, no special restriction on their power, because these acts are not the exercise of a power properly legislative. Their effect and object are to take away from one rights, property and franchises, and to grant them to another. This is not the exercise of a legislative power. To justify the taking away of vested rights there must be a forfeiture to adjudge upon and declare which is the proper province of the judiciary. Attainder and confiscation are acts of sovereign power, not acts of legislation. The British Parliament, among other unlimited powers, claims that of altering and vacating charters, not as an act of ordinary legislation, but of uncontrolled authority. It is theoretically omnipotent. Yet, in modern times, it has very rarely attempted the exercise of this power. In a celebrated instance those who asserted this power in Parliament vindicated its exercise only in a case in which it could be shown: First, that the charter in question was a charter of political power; second, that there was a great and overruling state necessity, justifying the violation of the charter; third, that the charter had been abused and justly forfeited. The bill affecting this charter did not pass. Its history is well known. The act which afterward did pass, passed *with the assent of the corporation.* Even in the worst times this power of Parliament to repeal and rescind charters has not often been exercised. The illegal proceedings in the reign of Charles II were under color of law. Judgments of forfeiture were obtained in the courts. Such was the case of the *quo warranto* against the city of London, and the proceedings by which the charter of Massachusetts was vacated.

The Legislature of New Hampshire has no power over the rights of the plaintiffs than existed somewhere in some department of government before the Revolution. The British Parliament could not have annulled or revoked this grant as an act of ordinary legislation. If it had done it at all it could only have been in virtue of that sovereign power, called omnipotent, which does not belong to any legislature in the United States. The Legislature of New Hampshire has the same power over this charter which belonged to the king who granted it, and no more. By the law of England the power to create corporations is a part of the royal prerogative. By the Revolution this power may be considered as having devolved on the legislature of the State, and it has accordingly been exercised by the legislature. But the king can not abolish a corporation, or new-model it, or alter its powers, without its assent. This is the acknowledged and well-known doctrine of the common law. "Whatever might have been the notion in former times," says Lords Mansfield, "it is most certain now that the corporations of the universities are lay corporations; and that the crown can not take away from them any rights that have been formerly subsisting in them under old charters or prescriptive usage.'' After forfeiture duly found, the king may regrant the franchises; but a grant of franchises already granted, and of which no forfeiture has been found, is void.

Corporate franchises can only be forfeited by trial and judgment. In case of a new charter or grant to an existing corporation it may accept or reject it as it pleases. It may accept such part of the grant as it chooses and reject the rest. In the very nature of things a charter can not be forced upon any body. No one can be compelled to accept a grant, and without acceptance the grant is necessarily void. It can not be pretended that the legislature, as successor to the king in this part of his prerogative, has any power to revoke, vacate, or alter this charter. If, therefore, the legislature has not this power, by any specific grant contained in the constitution, nor as included in the ordinary legislative powers, nor by reason of its succession to the prerogatives of the crown in this particular, on what ground would the authority to pass these acts rest, even if there were no prohibitory clauses in the constitution and the Bill of Rights?

But there *are prohibitions* in the Constitution and Bill of Rights of New Hampshire, introduced for the purpose of limiting the legislative power and protecting the rights and property of the citizens. One prohibition is, "that no person shall be deprived of his property, immunities, or privileges, put out of the protection of the law, or deprived of his life, liberty, or estate, but by judgment of his peers or the law of the land."

In the opinion, however, which was given in the court below, it is denied that the trustees under the charter had any property immunity, liberty, or privilege in this corporation within the meaning of this prohibition in the Bill of Rights. It is said that it is a public corporation and public property; that the trustees have no greater interest in it than any other individuals; that it is not private property which they can sell or transmit to their heirs, and that therefore they have no interest in it; that their office is a public trust, like that of the Governor or a judge, and that they have no more concern in the property of the college than the Governor in the property of the State, or than the judges in the fines which they impose on the culprits at their bar; that it is nothing to them whether their power shall be extended or lessened, any more than it is to their honors whether their jurisdiction shall be enlarged or diminished. It is necessary, therefore, to inquire into the true nature and character of the corporation which was created by the charter of 1769.

There are divers sorts of corporations; and it may be safely admitted that the legislature has more power over some than others. Some corporations are for government and political arrangement, as such, for example, as cities, counties, and towns in New England. These may be changed and modified as public conveniences may require, due regard being always had to the rights of property. Of such corporations, all who live within the limits are, of course, obliged to be members, and to submit to the duties which the law imposes on them as such. Other civil corporations are for the advancement of trade and business, such as banks, insurance companies, and the like. These are created, not by general law, but usually by grant. Their constitution is special. It is such as the legislature sees fit to give, and the grantees to accept.

The corporation in question is not a civil, altho it is a lay corporation. It is an eleemosynary corporation. It is a private charity, originally founded and endowed by an individual, with a charter obtained for it at his request, for the better administration of his charity. "The eleemosynary sort of corporations are such as are constituted for the perpetual distributions of the free alms or bounty of the founder of them to such persons as he has directed. Of this are all hospitals for the maintenance of the poor, sick and impotent; and all colleges, both in our universities and out of them." Eleemosynary corporations are for the management of private property, according to the will of the donors. They are private corporations. A college is as much a private corporation as a hospital; especially a college founded, as this was, by private bounty. A college is a charity. "The establishment of learning," says Lord Hardwicke, "is a charity, and so considered in the statute of Elizabeth. A devise to a college, for their benefit, is a laudable charity, and deserves encouragement."

The legal signification of a *charity* is derived chiefly from the statute 43 Eliz., ch. 4. "Those purposes," says Sir William Grant, "are considered *charitable* which that statute enumerates." Colleges are enumerated as charities in that statute. The government in these cases lends its aid to perpetuate the beneficent intention of the donor by granting a charter under which his private charity shall continue to be dispensed after his death. This is done either by incorporating the objects of the charity, as, for instance, the scholars in a college or the poor in a hospital, or by incorporating those who are to be governors or trustees of the charity. In cases of the first sort the founder is, by the common law, visitor. In early times it became a maxim, that he who gave the property might regulate it in future. "Cujus est dare, ejus est disponere." This right of visitation descended from the founder to his heir as a right of property, and precisely as his other property went to his heir; and in default of heirs it went to the king, as all other property goes to the king for the want of heirs. The right of visitation arises from the property. It grows out of the endowment. The founder may, if he pleases, part with it at any time when he establishes the charity, and may vest it in others. Therefore, if he chooses that governors, trustees, or overseers should be appointed in the charter, he may cause it to be done, and his power of visitation may be transferred to them, instead of descending to his heirs. The persons thus assigned or appointed by the founder will be visitors, with all the powers of the founder, in exclusion of his heirs. The right of visitation, then, accrues to them, as a matter of property, by the gift, transfer, or appointment of the founder. This is a private right, which they can assert in all legal modes, and in which they have the same protection of the law as in all other rights. As visitors they may make rules, ordinances, and statutes, and alter and repeal them, as far as permitted so to do by the charter. Altho the charter proceeds from the crown or the government, it is considered as the will of the donor. It is obtained at his request. He imposes it as the rule which is to prevail in the dispensation of his bounty in all future times. The king or government which grants the charter is not thereby the founder, but he who furnishes the funds. The gift of the revenues is the foundation.

The leading case on the subject is *Phillips v. Bury*. This was an ejectment brought to recover the rectory-house, etc., of Exeter College in Oxford. The question was whether the plaintiff or defendant was legal rector. Exeter College was founded by an individual, and incorporated by a charter granted by Queen Elizabeth. The controversy turned upon the power of the visitor, and, in the discussion of the cause, the nature of college charters and corporations was very fully considered. Lord Holt's judgment, copied from his own manuscript, is found in 2 Term Reports, 346. The following is an extract:

"That we may the better apprehend the nature of a visitor, we are to consider that there are in law two sorts of corporations aggregate; such as are for public government, and such as are for private charity. Those that are for the public government of a town, city, mystery, or the like, being for public advantage, are to be governed accordingly to the laws of the land. If they make any particular private laws and constitutions, the validity and justice of them is examinable in the king's courts. Of these there are no particular visitor; there are no patrons of these; therefore, if no provision be in the charter how the succession shall continue, the law supplieth the defect of the Constitution, and saith it shall be by election; as mayor, aldermen, common council, and the like. But *private* and particular corporations for charity, founded and endowed by private persons, are subject to the private government; if there be no visitor appointed by the founder, the law appoints the founder and his heirs to be visitors, who are to act and proceed according to the par-

STUDIES IN PROSE

ticular laws and constitutions assigned them by the founder. It is now admitted on all hands that the founder is patron, and as founder is visitor, if no particular visitor be assigned; so that patronage and visitation are necessary consequents, one upon another. For this visitorial power was not introduced by any canons or constitutions ecclesiastical (as was said by a learned gentleman whom I have in my eye, in his argument of this case); it is an appointment of law. It ariseth from the property which the founder had in the lands assigned to support the charity; and as he is the author of the charity, the law gives him and his heirs a visitatorial power, that is, an authority to inspect the actions and regulate the behavior of the members that partake of the charity. For it is fit the members that are endowed and that have the charity bestowed upon them, should not be left to themselves, but pursue the intent and design of him that bestowed it upon them. *Now, indeed, where the poor, or those that receive the charity, are not incorporated, but there are certain trustees who dispose of the charity, there is no visitor, because the interest of the revenue is not vested in the poor that have the benefit of the charity, but they are subject to the orders and directions of the trustees.* But where they who are to enjoy the benefit of the charity are incorporated, there to prevent all perverting of the charity, or to compose differences that may happen among them, there is by law a visitatorial power; and it being a creature of the founder's own, it is reason that he and his heirs should have that power, unless by the founder it is vested in some other. Now there is no manner of difference between a college and a hospital, except only in degree. A hospital is for those that are poor, and mean, and low, and sickly; a college is for another sort of indigent persons; but it hath another intent to study in and breed up persons in the world that have no otherwise to live; but still it is as much within the reasons as hospitals. And if in a hospital the master and poor are incorporated, it is a college having a common seal to act by, altho it hath not the name of a college (which always supposeth a corporation), because it is of an inferior degree; and in the one case and in the other there must be a visitor, either the founder and his heirs or one appointed by him; and both are eleemosynary.''

Lord Holt concluded his whole argument by again repeating that that college was a *private corporation,* and that the founder had a right to appoint a visitor, and give him such power as he saw fit.

The learned Bishop Stillingfleet's argument in the same cause as a member of the House of Lords, when it was there heard, exhibits very clearly the nature of colleges and similar corporations. It is to the following effect: ''That this absolute and conclusive power of visitors is no more than the law hath appointed in other cases, upon commission of charitable uses; that the common law, and not any ecclesiastical canons, do place the power of visitation in the founder and his heirs, *unless he settle it upon others;* that altho corporations for public government be subject to the courts of Westminster Hall, which have no particular or special visitors, yet corporations for charity founded and endowed by private persons, are subject to the rule and government of those that erect them; but where the persons to whom the charity is given are not incorporated, there is no such visitatorial power, because the interest of the revenue is not invested in them; but where they are, the right of visitation ariseth from the foundation, and the founder may convey it *to whom and in what manner he pleases; and the visitor acts as founder, and by the same authority which he had, and consequently is no more accountable than he had been;* that the king by his charter can make a society to be incorporated so as to have the rights belonging to persons, as to legal capacities; that colleges, altho founded by private persons, are yet incorporated by the king's charter; but altho the kings by their charter made the colleges to be such in law—that is, to be legal corporations—yet they left to the particular founders authority to appoint what statutes they thought fit for the regulation of them. And not only the statutes but the appointment of the visitors was left to them, and the manner of government, and the several conditions on which any persons were to be made or continue partakers of their bounty.''

These opinions received the sanction of the House of Lords, and they seem to be settled and undoubted law. Where there is a charter, vesting proper powers in trustees or governors, they are visitors; and there is no control in anybody else, except only that the courts of equity or of law will interfere so far as to preserve the revenues and prevent the perversion of the funds, and to keep the visitors within their prescribed bounds. "If there be a charter with proper powers, the charity must be regulated in the manner prescribed by the charter. There is no ground for the controlling interposition of the courts of chancery. The interposition of the courts, therefore, in those instances in which the charities were founded on charities or by act of Parliament, and a visitor or governor and trustees appointed, must be referred to the general jurisdiction of the courts in all cases in which a trust conferred appears to have been abused, and not to an original right to direct the management of the charity, or the conduct of the governors and trustees." "The original of all *visitatorial* power is the property of the donor, and the power every one has to dispose, direct, and regulate his own property, like the case of patronage; *cujus est dare*, etc. Therefore, if either the crown or the subject creates an eleemosynary foundation, and vests the charity in the persons who are to receive the benefit of it, since a contest might arise about the government of it, the laws allow the founder or his heirs, or the person specially appointed by him to be visitor, to determine concerning his own creature. If the charity is not vested in the persons who are to partake, but in trustees for their benefit, no visitor can arise by implication, but the trustees have that power."

"There is nothing better established," says Lord Commissioner Eyre, "than that this court does not entertain a general jurisdiction, or regulate and control charities *established by charter*. There the establishment is fixt and determined, and the court has no power to vary it. If the governors established for the regulation of it are not those who have the management of the revenue, that court has no jurisdiction, and if it is ever so much abused, as far as it respects the jurisdiction of this court, it is without remedy; but if those established as governors have also the management of the revenues, this court does assume a jurisdiction of necessity, so far as they are to be considered as trustees of the revenue."

"The foundations of colleges," says Lord Mansfield, "are to be considered in two views; namely, as they are *corporations* and as they are *eleemosynary*. As eleemosynary, they are the creatures of the founder; he may delegate his power, either generally or specially; he may prescribe particular modes and manners, as to the exercise of part of it. If he makes a general visitor (as by the general words *visitator sit*), the person so constituted has all incidental power; but he may be restrained as to particular instances. The founder may appoint a special visitor for a particular purpose, and no further. The founder may make a general visitor, and yet appoint an inferior particular power, to be executed without going to the visitor in the first instance." And even if the king be founder, if he grant a charter, incorporating trustees and governors, *they are visitors,* and the king can not visit. A subsequent donation or ingrafted fellowship falls under the same general visitatorial power, if not otherwise specially provided.

In New England, and perhaps throughout the United States, eleemosynary corporations have been generally established in the latter mode—that is, by incorporating governors, or trustees, and vesting in them the right of visitation. Small variations may have been in some instances adopted, as in the case of Harvard College, where some power of inspection is given to the overseers, but not, strictly speaking, a visitatorial power, which still belongs, it is apprehended, to the fellows or members of the corporation. In general, there are many donors. A charter is obtained, comprising them all, or some of them, and such others as they choose to include, with the right of appointing successors. They are thus the visitors of their own charity, and appoint others such as they may see fit, to exercise the same office in time to come. All such corporations are private. The case before the court is clearly that of an eleemosynary corporation. It is, in the strictest legal sense, a private charity. In *King v. St. Catherine's Hall,* that college is called a private eleemosynary lay corporation. It was endowed by a private founder, and incorporated by letters patent. And in the same manner was Dartmouth College founded and incorporated. Doctor Wheelock is declared by the charter to be its founder. It was established by him, on funds contributed and collected by himself.

As such founder he had a right of visitation, which he assigned to the trustees; and they received it by his consent and appointment, and held it under the charter. He appointed these trustees visitors, and in that respect to take place of his heir, as he might have appointed devisees to take his estate instead of his heir. Little, probably, did he think, at that time, that the legislature would ever take away this property and these privileges and give them to others. Little did he suppose that this charter secured to him and his successors no legal rights. Little did the other donors think so. If they had, the college would have been, what the university is now, a thing upon paper, existing only in name.

The numerous academies in New England have been established substantially in the same manner. They hold their property by the same tenure, and no other. Nor has Harvard College any surer title than Dartmouth College. It may to-day have more friends, but to-morrow it may have more enemies. So also of Yale College, and, indeed, of all the others. When the legislature gives to these institutions it may and does accompany its grants with such conditions as it pleases. The grant of lands by the Legislature of New England to Dartmouth College, in 1789, was accompanied with various conditions. When donations are made, by the legislature or others, to a charity already existing, without any condition or the specification of any new use, the donation follows the nature of the charity. Hence the doctrine, that all eleemosynary corporations are private bodies. They are founded by private persons, and on private property. The public can not be charitable in these institutions. It is not the money of the public, but of private persons, which is dispensed. It may be public—that is, general—in the uses and advantages; and the state may very laudably add contributions of its own to the funds; but it is still private in the tenure of the property and in the right of administering the funds.

If the doctrine laid down by Lord Holt and the House of Lords, *in Philips v. Bury,* and recognized and established in all the other cases, be correct, the property of this college was private property; it was vested in the trustees by the charter, and to be administered by them, according to the will of the founder and donors, as exprest in the charter. They were also visitors of the charity, in the most ample sense. They had, therefore, as they

STUDIES IN PROSE

contend, privileges, property and immunities, within the true meaning of the Bill of Rights. They had rights, and still have them, which they can assert against the legislature, as well as against other wrong-doers. It makes no difference that the estate is holden for certain trusts. The legal estate is still theirs. They have a right in the property, and they have a right of visiting and superintending the trust; and this is an object of legal protections as much as any other right. The charter declares that the powers conferred on the trustees are "privileges, advantages, liberties, and immunities"; and that they shall be forever holden by them and their successors. The New Hampshire Bill of Rights declares that no one shall be deprived of his "property, privileges, or immunities," but by judgment of his peers or the law of the land. The argument on the other side is, that, altho these terms may mean something in the Bill of Rights, they mean nothing in this charter. But they are terms of legal signification, and very properly used in the charter. They are equivalent with *franchises*. Blackstone says that *franchises* and *liberty* are used as synonymous terms. And after enumerating other liberties and franchises, he says: "It is likewise a franchise for a number of persons to be incorporated and subsist as a body politic, with a power to maintain perpetual succession and do other corporate acts; and each individual member of such a corporation is also said to have a franchise or freedom."

Liberties is the term used in Magna Charta as including franchises, privileges, immunities and all the rights which belong to that class. Professor Sullivan says the term signifies the "*privileges* that some of the subjects, whether single persons or bodies corporate, have above others by the lawful grant of the king; as the chattels of felons or outlaws, and the lands and *privileges of corporations.*"

The privilege, then, of being a member of a corporation under a lawful grant, and of exercising the rights and powers of such member, is such a privilege, *liberty,* or *franchise,* as has been the object of legal protection and the subject of legal interest from the time of Magna Charta to the present moment. The plaintiffs have such an interest in this corporation, individually, as they could assert and maintain in a court of law, not as agents of the public, but in their own right. Each trustee has a *franchise,* and if he be disturbed in the enjoyment of it he would have redress on appealing to the law as promptly as for any other injury. If the other trustees should conspire against any one of them to prevent his equal right and voice in the appointment of a president or professor, or in the passing of any statute or ordinance of the college, he would be entitled to his action, for depriving him of his franchise. It makes no difference that this property is to be holden and administered and these franchises exercised for the purpose of diffusing learning. No principle and no case establishes any such distinction. The public may be benefited by the use of this property. But this does not change the nature of the property or the rights of the owners. The object of the charter may be public good; so it is in all other corporations; and this would as well justify the resumption or violation of the grant in any other case as in this. In the case of an advowson, the use is public, and the right can not be turned to any private benefit or emolument. It is nevertheless a legal private right, and the *property* of the owner as emphatically as his freehold. The rights and privileges of trustees, visitors, or governors, of incorporated colleges, stand on the same foundation. They are so considered, both by Lord Holt and Lord Hardwicke.

To contend that the rights of the plaintiffs may be taken away because they derive from them no pecuniary benefit or private emolument, or because they can not be transmitted to their heirs, or would not be assets to pay their debts, is taking an extremely narrow view of the subject. According to this notion the case would be different if, in the charter, they had stipulated for a commission on the disbursement of the funds; and they have lost any interest in the property by having undertaken to administer it gratuitously.

It can not be necessary to say much in refutation of the idea that there can not be a legal interest or ownership in anything which does not yield a pecuniary profit, as if the law regarded no rights but the rights of money and of visible, tangible property. Of what nature are all rights of suffrage? No elector has a particular personal interest; but each has a legal right, to be exercised at his own discretion, and it can not be taken away from him. The exercise of this right directly and very materially affects the public, much more so than the exercise of the privileges of the trustees of this college. Consequences of the utmost magnitude may sometimes depend on the exercise of the right of suffrage by one or a few electors. Nobody was ever yet heard to contend, however, that on that account the public might take away the right or impair it. This notion appears to be borrowed from no better source than the repudiated doctrine of the three judges in the Aylesbury case. That was an action against a returning officer for refusing the plaintiff's vote in the election of a member of Parliament. Three of the judges of the King's Bench held that the action could not be maintained, because, among other objections, "it was not any matter of profit, either *in presenti,* or *in futuro.*" It would not enrich the plaintiff *in presenti,* nor would it *in futuro* go to his heirs, or answer to pay his debts. But Lord Holt and the House of Lords were of another opinion. The judgment of the three judges was reversed, and the doctrine they held, having been exploded for a century, seems now for the first time to be revived.

Individuals have a right to use their own property for purposes of benevolence, either toward the public or toward other individuals. They have a right to exercise this benevolence in such lawful manner as they may choose; and when the government has induced and excited it by contracting to give perpetuity to the stipulated manner of exercising it, it is not law but violence to rescind this contract and seize on the property. Whether the state will grant these franchises, and under what conditions it will grant them, it decides for itself. But when once granted the constitution holds them to be sacred till forfeited for just cause.

That all property, of which the use may be beneficial to the public, belongs therefore to the public, is quite a new doctrine. It has no precedent, and is supported by no known principle. Doctor Wheelock might have answered his purposes in this case by executing a private deed of trust. He might have conveyed his property to trustees for precisely such uses as are described in this charter. Indeed, it appears that he had contemplated the establishing of his school in that manner, and had made his will, and devised the property to the same persons who were afterward appointed trustees in the charter. Many literary and other charitable institutions are founded in that manner, and the trust is renewed, and conferred on other persons from time to time, as occasion may require. In such a case no lawyer would or could say that the legislature might divest the trustees, constituted by deed or will, seize upon the property, and give it to other persons, for other purposes. And does the granting of a charter, which is only done to perpetuate the trust in a more convenient manner, make any difference? Does or can this change the nature of the charity, and turn it into a public political corporation? Happily we are not without authority on the point. It has been considered and adjudged. Lord Hardwicke says, in so many words, "The charter of the crown can not make a charity more or less public, but only more permanent than it would otherwise be."

The granting of the corporation is but making the trust perpetual, and does not alter the nature of the charity. The very object sought in obtaining such charter, and in giving property to such a corporation, is to make and keep it private property, and to clothe it with all the security and inviolability of private property. The intent is, that there shall be a legal private ownership, and that the legal owners shall maintain and protect the property for the benefit of those for whose use it was designed. Who ever endowed the public? Who ever appointed a legislature to administer his charity? Or who ever heard before that a gift to a college, or a hospital, or an asylum was, in reality, nothing but a gift to the state?

The State of Vermont is a principal donor to Dartmouth College. The lands given lie in that State. This appears in the special verdict. Is Vermont to be considered as having intended a gift to the State of New Hampshire in this case, as, it has been said, is to be the reasonable construction of all donations to the college? The Legislature of New Hampshire affects to represent the public, and therefore claims a right to control all property destined to public use. What hinders Vermont from considering herself equally the representative of the public, and from resuming her grants at her own pleasure? Her right to do so is less doubtful than the power of New Hampshire to pass the laws in question.

In *University v. Foy*, the Supreme Court of North Carolina pronounced unconstitutional and void a law repealing a grant to the University of North Carolina, altho that university was originally erected and endowed by a statute of the State. That case was a grant of lands, and the court decided that it could not be resumed. This is the grant of a power and a capacity to hold lands. Where is the difference of the cases upon principle?

In *Terrett v. Taylor* this court decided that a legislative grant or confirmation of lands for the purpose of moral and religious instruction could no more be rescinded than other grants. The nature of the use was not holden to make any difference. A grant to a parish or church, for the purposes which have been mentioned, can not be distinguished, in respect to the title it confers, from a grant to a college for the promotion of piety and learning. To the same purpose may be cited the case of *Pawlett v. Clark*. The State of Vermont, by statute, in 1794, granted to the respective towns in that State certain glebe lands lying within those towns for the sole use and support of religious worship. In 1799 an act was passed to repeal the act of 1794, but this court declared that the act of 1794, "so far as it granted the glebes to the towns, could not afterward be repealed by the legislature, so as to divest the rights of the towns under the grant."

It will be for the other side to show that the nature of the use decides the question whether the legislature has the power to resume its grants. It will be for those who maintain such a doctrine to show the principles and cases upon which it rests. It will be for them also to fix the limits and boundaries of their doctrines, and to show what are and what are not such uses as to give the legislature this power of re-

STUDIES IN PROSE

sumption and revocation, and to furnish an answer to the cases cited, it will be for them further to show that a grant for the use and support of religious worship stands on other grounds than a grant for the promotion of piety and learning.

I hope enough has been said to show that the trustees possest vested liberties, privileges and immunities under this charter; and that such liberties, privileges and immunities, being once lawfully obtained and vested, are as inviolable as any vested rights of property whatever. Rights to do certain acts—such, for instance, as the visitation and superintendence of a college and the appointment of its officers—may surely be vested rights, to all legal intents, as completely as the right to possess property. A late learned judge of this court has said, "When I say that a *right* is vested in a citizen, I mean that he has the power to do *certain actions*, or to possess *certain things*, according to the law of the land."

If such be the true nature of the plaintiffs' interests under this charter, what are the articles in the New Hampshire Bill of Rights these acts infringe?

They infringe the second article, which says that the citizens of the State have a right to hold and possess property. The plaintiffs had a legal property in this charter, and they had acquired property under it. The acts deprive them of both. They impair and take away the character; and they appropriate the property to new uses against their consent. The plaintiffs can not now hold the property acquired by themselves, and which this article says they have a right to hold.

They infringe the twentieth article. By that article it is declared that, in questions of property, there is a right to trial. The plaintiffs are divested without trial or judgment.

They infringe the twenty-third article. It is therein declared that no retrospective laws shall be passed. This article bears directly on the case. These acts must be deemed to be retrospective, within the settled construction of that term. What a retrospective law is has been decided, on the construction of this very article, in the Circuit Court for the First Circuit. The learned judge of that circuit says: "Every statute which takes away or impairs vested rights, acquired under existing laws, must be deemed retrospective." That all such laws are retrospective was decided also in the case of *Dash v. Van Kleek*, where a most learned judge quotes this article from the Constitution of New Hampshire, with manifest approbation, as a plain and clear expression of those fundamental and unalterable principles of justice which must lie at the foundation of every free and just system of laws. Can any man deny that the plaintiffs had rights under the charter which were legally vested, and that by these acts those rights are impaired?

"It is a principle in the English law," says Chief Justice Kent, in the case last cited, "as ancient as the law itself, that a statute, even of its omnipotent Parliament, is not to have a retrospective effect. 'Nova Constitutio futuris formam imponere debet, et non præteritis.' The maxim in Bracton was taken from the civil law, for we find in that system the same principle, exprest substantially in the same words, that the law-giver can not alter his mind to the prejudice of a vested right. 'Nemo potest mutare concilium suum in alterius injuriam.' This maxim of Papinian is general in its terms, but Doctor Taylor applies it directly as a restriction upon the law-giver, and a declaration in the code leaves no doubt as to the sense of the civil law. 'Leges et constitutiones futuris certum est dare formam negotiis, non ad facta præterita revocari, nisi nominatim, et de præterito tempore, et adhuc pendentibus negotiis cautum sit.' This passage, according to the best interpretation of the civilians, relates not merely to future suits, but to future, as contradistinguished from past, contracts and vested rights. It is, indeed, admitted that the prince may enact a retrospective law, provided it be done *expressly;* for the will of the prince under the despotism of the Roman emperors was paramount to every obligation. Great latitude was anciently allowed to legislative expositions of statutes, for the separation of the judicial from the legislative power was not then distinctly known or prescribed. The prince was in the habit of interpreting his own laws for particular occasions. This was called the 'Interlocutio Principis,' and this, according to Huber's definition, was 'Quando principes inter partes loquuntur et jus dicunt.' No correct civilian, and especially no proud admirer of the ancient republic (if any such then existed), could have reflected on this interference with private rights and pending suits without disgust and indignation; and we are rather surprised to find that, under the violent and arbitrary genius of the Roman Government, the principle before us should have been acknowledged and obeyed to the extent in which we find it. The fact shows that it must be founded in the clearest justice. Our case is happily very different from that of the subjects of Justinian. With us the power of the law-giver is limited and defined; the judicial is regarded as a distinct, independent power; private rights are better understood and more exalted in public estimation, as well as secured by provisions dictated by the spirit of freedom, and unknown to the civil law. Our constitutions do not admit the power assumed by the Roman princes, and the principle we are considering is now to be regarded as sacred."

These acts infringe also the thirty-seventh article of the Constitution of New Hampshire, which says that the powers of government shall be kept separate. By these acts the legislature assumes to exercise a judicial power. It declares a forfeiture and resumes franchises, once granted, without trial or hearing.

If the constitution is not altogether wastepaper, it has restrained the power of the legislature in these particulars. If it has any meaning, it is that the legislature shall pass no act directly, and manifestly impairing private property and private privileges. It shall not judge by act. It shall not decide by act. But it shall leave all these things to be tried and adjudged by the laws of the land.

The fifteenth article has been referred to before. It declares that no one shall be "deprived of his property, immunities, or privileges, but by the judgment of his peers or the law of the land." Notwithstanding the light in which the learned judges in New Hampshire viewed the rights of the plaintiffs under the charter, and which has before been adverted to, be admitted to their opinion that those rights are privileges within the fifteenth article of the Bill of Rights. Having quoted that article, they say, "That the right to manage the affairs of this college is a privilege, within the meaning of this clause of the Bill of Rights, is not to be doubted." In my humble opinion, this surrenders the point. To resist the effect of this admission, however, the learned judges add: "But how a privilege can be protected from the operation of the law of the land by a clause in the constitution declaring that it shall not be taken away but by the law of the land, is not very easily understood." This answer goes on the ground that the acts in question are laws of the land within the meaning of the constitution. If they be so, the argument drawn from this article is fully answered. If they be not so, it being admitted that the plaintiffs' rights are "privileges," within the meaning of the article, the argument is not answered, and the article is infringed by the acts.

Are, then, these acts of the legislature which affect only particular persons and their particular privileges, laws of the land? Let this question be answered by the text of Blackstone. "And first it (*i.e.*, law) is a *rule*—not a transient, sudden order from a superior to or concerning a particular person, but something permanent, uniform and universal. Therefore, a particular act of the legislature to confiscate the goods of Titus, or to attaint him of high treason, does not enter into the idea of a municipal law, for the operation of this act is spent upon Titus only, and has no relation to the commnity in general; it is rather a sentence than a law." Lord Coke is equally decisive and emphatic. Citing and commenting on the celebrated twenty-ninth chapter of Magna Charta, he says: "No

STUDIES IN PROSE

man shall be disseized, etc., unless it be by the lawful judgment, that is, verdict of equals, or by the law of the land, that is (to speak it once for all), by the due course and process of law." Have the plaintiffs lost their franchises by "due course and process of law?" On the contrary, are not these acts "particular acts of the legislature, which have no relation to the community in general, and which are rather sentences than laws?"

By the law of the land is most clearly intended the general law, a law which hears before it condemns, which proceeds upon inquiry, and renders judgment only after trial. The meaning is, that every citizen shall hold his life, liberty, property and immunities under the protection of the general rules which govern society. Everything which may pass under the form of an enactment is not therefore to be considered the law of the land. If this were so, acts of the attainer, bills of pains and penalties, acts of confiscation, acts of reversing judgments, and acts directly transferring one man's estate to another, legislative judgments, decrees, and forfeitures in all possible forms, would be the law of the land.

Such a strange construction would render constitutional provisions of the highest importance completely inoperative and void. It would tend directly to establish the union of all powers in the legislature. There would be no general, permanent law for courts to administer or men to live under. The administration of justice would be an empty form. "Is that the law of the land," says Mr. Burke, "upon which, if a man go to Westminster Hall, and ask counsel by what title of tenure he holds his privilege or estate *according to the law of the land,* he should be told that the law of the land is not yet known; that no decision or decree has been made in his case; that when a decree shall be passed, he will then know *what the law of the land is?* Will this be said to be the law of the land by any lawyer who has a rag of a gown left upon his back or a wig with one tie upon his head?"

That the power of electing and appointing the officers of this college is not only a right of the trustees as a corporation, generally and in the aggregate, but that each individual trustee has also his own individual franchise in such rights of election and appointment, is according to the language of all the authorities. Lord Holt says: "It is agreeable to reason and the rules of law that a franchise should be vested in the corporation aggregate, and yet the benefit of it to redound to the particular members, and to be enjoyed by them in their private capacity. Where the privilege of election is used by particular persons, it is a *particular right vested in every particular man.*"

It is also to be considered, that the president and professors of this college have rights to be affected by these acts. Their interest is similar to that of fellows in the English colleges, because they derive their living, wholly or in part, from the founders' bounty. The president is one of the trustees or corporators. The professors are not necessarily members of the corporation; but they are appointed by the trustees, and removable by them, and have fixt salaries payable out of the general funds of the college. Both president and professors have freeholds in their offices, subject only to be removed by the trustees, as their legal visitors, for good cause. All the authorities speak of fellowships in colleges as freeholds, notwithstanding the fellows may be liable to be suspended or removed for misbehavior by their constituted visitors.

Nothing could have been less expected in this age than that there should have been an attempt, by acts of the legislature, to take away these college livings, the inadequate but the only support of literary men who have devoted their lives to the instruction of youth. The president and professors were appointed by the twelve trustees. They were accountable to nobody else, and could be removed by nobody else. They accepted their offices on this tenure. Yet the legislature has appointed other persons, with power to remove these officers and to deprive them of their livings, and those other persons have exercised that power. No description of private property has been regarded as more sacred than college livings. They are the estates and freeholds of a most deserving class of men, of scholars who have consented to forego the advantages of professional and public enjoyments, and to devote themselves to science and literature and the instruction of youth in the quiet retreats of academic life. Whether to dispossess and oust them, to deprive them of their office, and to turn them out of their livings; to do this, not by the power of their legal visitors or governors, but by acts of the legislature, and to do it without forfeiture and without fault; whether all this be not in the highest degree an indefensible and arbitrary proceeding, is a question of which there would seem to be but one side for a lawyer or a scholar to espouse.

Of all the attempts of James II to overturn the law and the rights of his subjects, none was esteemed more arbitrary or tyrannical than his attack on Magdalen College, Oxford; and yet that attempt was nothing but to put out one president and put in another. The president of that college, according to the charter and statutes, is to be chosen by the fellows who are the corporators. There being a vacancy, the king chose to take the appointment out of the hands of the fellows, the legal electors of a president, into his own hands. He therefore sent down his mandate, commanding the fellows to admit for president a person of his nomination; and, inasmuch as this was directly against the charter and constitution of the college, he was pleased to add a *non obstante* clause of sufficiently comprehensive import. The fellows were commanded to admit the person mentioned in the mandate, "any statute, custom or constitution to the contrary notwithstanding, wherewith we are graciously pleased to dispense in this behalf." The fellows refused obedience to this mandate, and Doctor Hough, a man of independence and character, was chosen president by the fellows, according to the charter and statutes. The king then assumed the power, in virtue of his prerogative, to send down certain commissioners to turn him out, which was done accordingly, and Parker, a creature suited to the times, put in his place. Because the president, who was rightfully and legally elected, *would not deliver the keys the doors were broken open.* "The nation as well as the university," says Bishop Burnet, "looked on all these proceedings with just indignation. It was thought an open piece of robbery and burglary when men, authorized by no legal commission, came and forcibly turned men out of their possession and freehold." Mr. Hume, altho a man of different temper and of other sentiments, in some respects, than Doctor Burnet, speaks of this arbitrary attempt of prerogative in terms not less decisive. "The president, and all the fellows," says he, "except two, who complied, were expelled the college, and Parker was put in possession of the office. This act of violence, of all those which were committed during the reign of James, is perhaps the most illegal and arbitrary. When the dispensing power was the most strenuously insisted on by court lawyers, it had still been allowed that the statutes which regard private property could not legally be infringed by that prerogative. Yet, in this instance, it appeared that even these were not now secured from invasion. The privileges of a college are attacked; men are illegally dispossest of their property for adhering to their duty, to their oaths, and to their religion."

This measure King James lived to repent, after repentance was too late. When the charter of London was restored the other measures of violence were retracted to avert the impending revolution; the expelled president and fellows of Magdalen College were permitted to resume their rights. It is evident that this was regarded as an arbitrary interference with private property. Yet private property was not otherwise attacked than as a person was appointed to administer and enjoy the revenues of a college in a manner and by persons not authorized by the constitution of the college. A majority of the members of the corporation would not comply with the king's wishes. A minority would. The object was, therefore, to make this minority a majority. To this end the king's commissioners were directed to interfere in the case, and they united with the two complying fellows and expelled the rest, and thus effected a change in the government of the college. The language in which Mr. Hume and all the other writers speak of this abortive attempt of oppression shows that colleges were esteemed to be, as they truly are, private corporations, and the property and privileges which belong to them *private* property and *private* privileges. Court lawyers were found to justify the king in dispensing with the laws—that is, in assuming and exercising a legislative authority. But no lawyer, not even a court lawyer in the reign of King James II, as far as appears, was found to say that, even by this high authority, he could infringe the franchise of the fellows of the college and take away their livings. Mr. Hume gives the reason: It is, that such franchise were regarded in a most emphatic sense as *private property*. If it could be made to appear that the trustees and the president and professors held their offices and franchises during the pleasure of the legislature, and that the property holden belonged to the State, then the legislature have done no more than they had a right to do. But this is not so. The charter is a charter of privileges and immunities; and these are holden by the trustees expressly against the State forever.

It is admitted that the State, by its courts of law, can enforce the will of the donor, and compel a faithful execution of the trust. The plaintiffs claim no exemption from legal responsibility. They hold themselves at all times answerable to the law of the land for their conduct in the trust committed to them. They ask only to hold the property of which they are owners, and the franchises which belong to them, until they shall be found, by due course and process of law, to have forfeited them.

It can make no difference whether the legislature exercises the power it has assumed by removing the trustees and the president and the professors, directly and by name, or by appointing others to expel them. The principle is the same, and in the point of fact the result has been the same. If the entire franchise can not be taken away, neither can it be essentially impaired. If the trustees are legal owners of the property, they are sole owners. If they are visitors, they are sole visitors. No one will be found to say that, if the legislature may do what it has done, it may not do anything and everything which it may choose to do, relative to the property of the corporation and the privileges of the members and officers.

If the view which has been taken of this

question be at all correct, this was an eleemosynary corporation, a private charity. The property was private property. The trustees were visitors, and the right to hold the charter, administer the funds and visit and govern the college was a franchise and privilege, solemnly granted to them. The use being public in no way diminishes their legal estate in the property, or their title to the franchise. There is no principle, nor any case, which declares that a gift to such a corporation is a gift to the public. The acts in question violate property. They take away privileges, immunities and franchises. They deny to the trustees the protection of the law; and they are retrospective in their operation. In all which respects they are against the Constitution of New Hampshire.

The plaintiffs contend, in the second place, that the acts in question are repugnant to the tenth section of the first article of the Constitution of the United States. The material words of that section are: "No State shall pass any bill of attainder, *ex post facto* law, or law impairing the obligation of contracts."

The object of these most important provisions in the national Constitution has often been discust, both here and elsewhere. It is exhibited with great clearness and force by one of the distinguished persons who framed that instrument. "Bills of attainder, *ex post facto* laws, and laws impairing the obligation of contracts, are contrary to the first principles of sound legislation. The two former are expressly prohibited by the declaration prefixt to some of the State constitutions, and all of them prohibited by the spirit and scope of these fundamental charters. Our own experiences have taught us, nevertheless, that additional fences against these dangers ought not to be omitted. Very properly, therefore, have the convention added this constitutional bulwark in favor of personal security and private rights; and I am much deceived if they have not in so doing as faithfully consulted the genuine sentiments as the undoubted interests of their constituents. The sober people of America are weary of the fluctuating policy which has directed the public councils. They have seen with regret and with indignation that sudden changes and legislative interferences in cases affecting personal rights become jobs in the hands of enterprising and influential speculators and snares to the more industrious and less informed part of the community. They have seen, too, that one legislative interference is but the link of a long chain of repetitions; every subsequent interference being naturally produced by the effects of the proceeding.''

It has already been decided in this court that a *grant* is a contract, within the meaning of this provision; and that a grant by a State is also a contract, as much as the grant of an individual. In the case of *Fletcher v. Peck*, this court says: "A contract is a compact between two or more parties, and is either executory or executed. An executory contract is one in which a party binds himself to do, or not to do, a particular thing; such was the law under which the conveyance was made by the government. A contract executed is one in which the object of the contract is performed; and this, says Blackstone, differs in nothing from a grant. The contract between Georgia and the purchasers was executed, as well as one which is executory, contains obligations binding on the parties. A grant, in its own nature amounts to an extinguishment of the right of grantor, and implies a contract not to reassert that right. If, under a fair construction of the constitution, grants are comprehended under the term contracts, is a grant from the State excluded from the operation of the provision? Is this clause to be considered as inhibiting the State from impairing the obligation of contracts between two individuals, but as excluding from that inhibition contracts made with itself? The words themselves contain no such distinction. They are general, and are applicable to contracts made with the State, and are to be exempted from their operation; the exception must arise from the character of the contracting party, not from the words which are employed. Whatever respect might have been felt for the State sovereignties, it is not to be disguised that the framers of the Constitution viewed with some apprehension the violent acts which might grow out of the feeling of the moment; and that the people of the United States, in adopting that instrument, have manifested a determination to shield themselves and their property from the effects of those sudden and strong passions to which men are exposed. The restrictions on the legislative power of the States are obviously founded in this sentiment; and the Constitution of the United States contains what may be deemed a bill of rights for the people of each State. It has also been decided that a grant by a State before the Revolution is as much to be protected as a grant since. But the case of *Terrett v. Taylor,* before cited, is of all others most pertinent to the present argument. Indeed, the judgment of the court in that case seems to leave little to be argued or decided in this. "A private corporation," says the court, "created by the legislature may lose its franchises by a *misuser* or a *nonuser* of them; and they may be resumed by the government under a judicial judgment upon a *quo warranto* to ascertain and enforce the forfeiture. This is the common law of the land, and is a tacit condition annexed to the creation of every such corporation. Upon a change of govern-

STUDIES IN PROSE

ment, too, it may be admitted, that such exclusive privileges attached to a private corporation as are inconsistent with the new government may be abolished. In respect also to *public* corporations which exist only for public purposes, such as counties, towns, cities, and so forth, the legislature may, under proper limitations, have a right to change, modify, enlarge, or restrain them, securing, however, the property for the uses of those for whom and at whose expense it was originally purchased. But that the legislature can repeal statutes creating private corporations, or confirming to them property already acquired under the faith of previous laws, and by such repeal can vest the property of such corporations exclusively in the State, or dispose of the same to purposes as they please, without the consent or default of the corporators, we are not prepared to admit; and we think ourselves standing upon the principles of natural justice, upon the fundamental laws of every free government, upon the spirit and the letter of the Constitution of the United States, and upon the decisions of most respectable judicial tribunals, in resisting such a doctrine.''

This court, then, does not admit the doctrine that a legislature can repeal statutes creating private corporations. If it can not repeal them altogether, of course, it can not repeal any part of them, or impair them, or essentially alter them, without the consent of the corporators. If, therefore, it has shown that this college is to be regarded as a private charity, this case is embraced within the very terms of that decision. A grant of corporate powers and privileges is as much a contract as a grant of land. What proves all charters of this sort to be contracts is, that they must be accepted to give them force and effect. If they are not accepted they are void. And in the case of an existing corporation, if a new charter is given it, it may even accept part and reject the rest. In *Rex. v. Vice-Chancellor of Cambridge*, Lord Mansfield says: "There is a vast deal of difference between a new charter granted to a new corporation (who must take it as it is given) and a new charter given to a corporation already in being, and acting either under a former charter or under prescriptive usage. The latter, a corporation already existing, are not obliged to accept the new charter *in toto*, and to receive either all or none of it; they must act partly under it, and partly under their old charter or prescription. The validity of these new charters must turn upon the acceptance of them." In the same case Mr. Justice Wilmot says: "It is the concurrence and acceptance of the university that gives the force to the charter of the crown." In the *King v. Pasmore*, Lord Kenyon observes: "Some things are clear: When a corporation exists capable of discharging its functions, the crown can not obtrude another charter upon them; they may either accept or reject it."

In all cases relative to charters, the acceptance of them is uniformly alleged in the pleadings. This shows the general understanding of the law, that they are grants or contracts, and that parties are necessary to give them force and validity. In *King v. Dr. Askew*, it is said, "The crown can not oblige a man to be a corporator without his consent; he shall not be subject to the inconveniences of it without accepting it and assenting to it." These terms, "acceptance" and "assent," are the very language of contract. In *Ellis v. Marshall* it is expressly adjudged that the naming of the defendant among others, in an act of incorporation, did not of itself make him a corporator; and that his assent was necessary to that end. The court speaks of the act of incorporation as a grant, and observes, "That a man may refuse a grant, whether from the government or an individual, seems to be a principle too clear to require the support of authorities." But Justice Buller, in *King v. Pasmore*, furnishes, if possible, a still more direct and explicit authority. Speaking of a corporation for government, he says: "I do not know how to reason on this point better than in the manner urged by one of the relator's counsel, who considered the grant of incorporation to be a compact between the crown and a certain number of the subjects, the latter of whom undertake, in consideration of the privileges which are bestowed to exert themselves for the good government of the place." This language applies with peculiar propriety and force to the case before the court. It was in consequence of the "privileges bestowed" that Doctor Wheelock and his associates undertook to exert themselves for the instruction and education of youth in this college; and it was on the same consideration that the founder endowed it with his property.

And because charters of incorporation are of the nature of contracts, they can not be altered or varied but by consent of the original parties. If a charter be granted by the king, it may be altered by a new charter granted by the king, and accepted by the corporators. But if the first charter be granted by Parliament, the consent of Parliament must be obtained to any alteration. In *King v. Miller,* Lord Kenyon says, "Where a corporation takes its rise from the king's charter, the king by granting, and the corporation by accepting another charter may alter it, because it is done with the consent of all parties who are competent to consent to the alteration."

There are, in this case, all the essential constituent parts of a contract. There is something to be contracted about. There are parties, and there are plain terms in which the argument of the parties on the subject of the contract is exprest. There are mutual considerations and inducements. The charter recites that the founder, on his part, has agreed to establish his seminary in New Hampshire, and to enlarge it beyond its original design, among other things, for the benefit of that province; and thereupon a charter is given to him and his associates, designated by himself, promising and assuring to them, under the plighted faith of the State, the right of governing the college and administering its concerns in the manner provided in the charter. There is a complete and perfect grant to them of all the power of superintendence, visitation and government. Is not this a contract? If lands or money had been granted to him and his associates for the same purposes, such grant could not be rescinded. And is there any difference in legal contemplation between a grant of corporate franchises and a grant of tangible property? No such difference is recognized in any decided case, nor does it exist in the common apprehension of mankind.

It is therefore contended that this case falls within the true meaning of this provision of the Constitution, as expounded in the decisions of this court; that the charter of 1769 is a contract, a stipulation or agreement, mutual in its considerations, express and formal in its terms, and of a most binding and solemn nature. That the acts in question impair this contract has already been sufficiently shown. They repeal and abrogate its most essential parts.

A single observation may not be improper on the opinion of the court of New Hampshire, which has been published. The learned judges who delivered that opinion have viewed this question in a very different light from that in which the plaintiffs have endeavored to exhibit it. After some general remarks, they assume that this college is a public corporation, and on this basis their judgment rests. Whether all colleges are not regarded as private and eleemosynary corporations by all law writers and all judicial decisions; whether this college was not founded by Doctor Wheelock; whether the charter was not granted at his request, the better to execute a trust, which he had already created; whether he and his associates did not become visitors by the charter; and whether Dartmouth College be not, thereof, in the strictest sense, a private charity, are questions which the learned judges do not appear to have discust.

It is admitted in that opinion that, if it be a private corporation, its rights stand on the same ground as those of an individual. The great question, therefore, to be decided is, to which class of corporations do colleges thus founded belong? And the plaintiffs have endeavored to satisfy the court that, according to the well-settled principles and uniform decisions of law, they are private, eleemosynary corporations.

Much has heretofore been said on the necessity of admitting such power in the legislature as has been assumed in this case. Many cases of possible evil have been imagined, which might otherwise be without remedy. Abuses, it is contended, might arise in the management of such institutions which the ordinary courts of law would be unable to correct. But this is only another instance of that habit of supposing extreme cases, and then of reasoning from them, which is the constant refuge of those who are obliged to defend a cause which, upon its merits, is indefensible. It would be sufficient to say in answer that it is not pretended that there was here any such case of necessity. But a still more satisfactory answer is that the apprehension of danger is growing less, and therefore the whole argument fails. Experience has not taught us that there is danger of great evils or of great inconvenience from this source. Hitherto, neither in our own country nor elsewhere have such cases of necessity occurred. The judicial establishment of the State are presumed to be competent to prevent abuses and violations of trust, in cases of this kind as well as in others. If they be not, they are imperfect, and their amendment would be a most proper subject for legislative wisdom. Under the government and protection of the general laws of the land these institutions have always been found safe, as well as useful. They go on, with the progress of society, accommodating themselves easily, without sudden change or violence, to the alternations which take place in its condition, and in the knowledge, the habits and pursuits of men. The English colleges were founded in Catholic ages. Their religion was reformed with the general reformation of the nation; and they are suited perfectly well to the purpose of educating the Protestant youth of modern times. Dartmouth College was established under a charter granted by the Provincial Government; but a better constitution for a college, or one more adapted to the condition of things under the present government, in all material respects, could not now be framed. Nothing in it was found to need alteration at the Revolution. The wise men of that day saw in it one of the best hopes of future times, and commended it as it was, with parental care, to the protection and guardianship of the government of the State. A charter of more liberal sentiments, of wiser provisions drawn with more care, or in a better spirit, could not be expected at any time or from any source. The college needed no change in its organization or government.

STUDIES IN PROSE

That which it did need was the kindness, the patronage, the bounty of the legislature; not a mock elevation to the character of a university, without the solid benefit of a shilling's donation to sustain the character; not the swelling and empty authority of establishing institutes and other colleges. This unsubstantial pageantry would seem to have been in derision of the scanty endowment and limited means of an unobtrusive but useful and growing seminary. Least of all was there a necessity, or pretense of necessity, to infringe its legal rights, violate its franchises and privileges, and pour upon it these overwhelming streams of litigation.

But this argument from necessity would equally apply in all other cases. If it be well founded, it would prove that, whenever any inconvenience or evil is experienced from the restrictions imposed on the legislature by the Constitution, these restrictions ought to be disregarded. It is enough to say that the people have thought otherwise. They have, most wisely, chosen to take the risk of occasional inconvenience from the want of power, in order that there might be a settled limit to its exercise and a permanent security against its abuse. They have imposed prohibitions and restraints; and they have not rendered these altogether vain and nugatory by conferring the power of dispensation. If inconvenience should arise which the legislature can not remedy under the power conferred upon it, it is not answerable for such inconvenience. That which it can not do within the limits prescribed to it, it can not do at all. No legislature in this country is able—and may the time never come when it shall be able—to apply to itself the memorable expression of a Roman pontiff: *"Licet hoc de jure non possumus, volumus tamen de plenitudine potestatis."*

The case before the court is not of ordinary importance nor of every-day occurrence. It has a wide-spread and vital interest. It affects not this college only, but every college, and all the literary institutions of the country. They have flourished hitherto, and have become in a high degree respectable and useful to the community. They have all a common principle of existence, the inviolability of their charters. It will be a dangerous, a most dangerous experiment, to hold these institutions subject to the rise and fall of popular parties and the fluctuations of political opinions. If the franchise may be at any time taken away or impaired, the property also may be taken away or its use perverted. Benefactors will have no certainty of effecting the object of their bounty, and learned men will be deterred from devoting themselves to the service of such institutions from the precarious title of their offices. Colleges and halls will be deserted by all better spirits and become a theater for the contentions of politics. Party and faction will be cherished in the places consecrated to piety and learning. These consequences are neither remote nor possible only. They are certain and immediate.

When the court in North Carolina declared the law of the State, which repealed a grant to its university, unconstitutional and void, the legislature had the candor and the wisdom to repeal the law. This example, so honorable to the State which exhibited it, is most fit to be followed on this occasion. And there is good reason to hope that a State, which has hitherto been so much distinguished for temperate counsels, cautious legislation and regard to law, will not fail to adopt a course which will in every respect most completely accord with her highest, noblest, and best interests, and in no small degree elevate her reputation.

It was for many and obvious reasons most anxiously desired that the question of the power of the legislature over this charter should have been finally decided in the State court. An earnest hope was entertained that the judges of the court might have viewed the case in a light favorable to the rights of the trustees. This hope has failed. It is here that those rights are now to be maintained, or they are prostrated forever. "Omnia alia perfugia bonorum, subsidia, consilia, auxilia, jura ceciderunt. Quem enim alium appellem? quem obtester? quem implorem? Nisi hoc loco, nisi apud vos, nisi per vos, judices, salutem nostram, quæ spe exigua extremaque pendet, tenuerimus; nihil est præterea quo confugere possimus."

WILLIAM PITT, EARL OF CHATHAM

BY THOMAS CARLYLE

WILLIAM PITT, Earl of Chatham, the second son of Robert Pitt, Esq., of Boconnock, in the county of Cornwall, was born on the 15th of November, 1708. The family was originally of Blandford, in Dorsetshire. Christopher Pitt, the translator of Vida and Vergil, and Thomas Pitt, Governor of Madras in the reign of Queen Anne, were both of this place. The latter was Chatham's grandfather, and likewise remarkable as having purchased, during his residence in the East, the jewel known by the name of the Pitt Diamond, which weighed 127 carats, and was afterward sold by him to the King of France for 135,000 lire, having originally cost 20,400 lire. It may also be worthy of mention that, by the wife of this gentleman, Chatham was descended from the Regent Murray, natural son of James V of Scotland.

Of Chatham's youth and early habits little is recorded, except that he studied at Eton as a foundation-scholar; was removed to Trinity College, Oxford, in 1726, and left the university without taking any degree. His proficiency in the attainments usually acquired there may, however, be inferred from the circumstance that some Latin verses of his were judged fit to appear in the collection printed by that learned body on the death of George I; and still more, certainly, from the predilection for classical pursuits which he displayed in after life, and the decidedly classical tincture which pervades all his compositions. Demosthenes is said to have been so great a favorite with him that he repeatedly translated certain of his orations into English.

The immediate cause of his removal from Oxford was a hereditary gout, which had already attacked him at Eton in his sixteenth year. He sought to expel the disorder by traveling. He made the tour of France, and visited Italy, but without realizing his purpose; his gout still adhered to him, it preyed upon his constitution throughout life, and never left him till it gained the mastery. To an ordinary mind this malady would have proved a severe misfortune; Pitt found means to convert it into almost an advantage. Excluded by it from the gayeties and dissipations of common life, he applied himself the more earnestly to the acquisition of knowledge. He read, and wrote, and studied, endeavoring by every method in his power to cultivate those faculties which were one day to become the ornament of his age and nation.

In the meantime, however, his immediate prospects were by no means magnificent. He had lost his father in 1727; a scanty fortune and a sickly frame made him anxious for some fixt appointment; and he was glad to accept a commission of cornet in the Blues, which some of his friends had interest enough to procure for him. But his inclinations pointed to a different scene. The leisure which his duties left him was still sedulously consecrated to the improvement of his mind, and he longed to employ in public life those talents he had been so careful to perfect. In 1735 this opportunity was granted him. He was that year returned member for Old Sarum, to serve in the Ninth Parliament of Great Britain. The appearance he made there was such as to justify all his hopes and to awaken hopes still more glorious. His eloquence soon became the pride of his friends and the terror of all that opposed him. A fine voice and figure prepossest the hearers in his favor, and the sentiments and opinions which he uttered bespoke a great and noble mind. There was in him a stern, inexpiable contempt for meanness in whatever shape; a fervid enthusiasm for the cause of freedom, for the honor of his country, for all good and worthy things; the whole tempered and matured by a strong, commanding intellect, the force and justness of which might have seemed scarcely compatible with so much youthful ardor. His acquired advantages gave full scope to those gifts of nature. The style he employed was chaste, regular and argumentative, yet both splendid and impassioned, and the energetic graces of his delivery gave new power to what he spoke. When warmed with his subject, when pouring forth his own glowing feelings and emphatic convictions, in language as glowing and emphatic, the attitude of conscious strength which he assumed, his lofty looks, his indignant glance, would dismay the stoutest and most subtle of his opponents; and the veterans of Parliament have stood abashed in the presence of a youth. Sir Robert Walpole, in his pride of place, with all the dexterity of ministerial management which a life had been spent in acquiring, was awed before this champion of simple virtue. Detected in his sophistries, stigmatized for his corruptions, baffled in his attempts at retaliation or defense, this intriguing statesman came at length to dread, as the signal of defeat, the very sound of his adversary's voice. "Let us before all things," said he, "try to muzzle this terrible cornet of horse."

But the enterprise was ineffectual, the cornet was not to be "muzzled"; and if Sir Robert still believed in his favorite maxim, that every man has his price, it must have mortified him to discover that the price of Pitt was not within the compass of his gift. Unable to gain over, he took the imperfect satisfaction of alienating still further. Pitt was deprived of his commission in the army;

and this stroke of official severity, while it confirmed him in his opposition, rendered him still dearer to the public, whose rights he was asserting. It strengthened him also in the favor of Frederick, Prince of Wales, the center at that period of all who aimed at a change of men and measures. Pitt was appointed groom of the bed-chamber to the prince in the year 1737. He continued in the successive sessions of Parliament to support the same liberal principles which he had at first adopted, the increase of years increasing his experience in the principles of policy and government without seeming to abate the ardor of his zeal. He distinguished himself by his animated hostility to the Spanish Convention in 1738, and generally by his aversion to every measure that appeared likely to injure the rights of the subject or the lasting interests of the country. His speeches contributed not a little to the downfall of Sir Robert Walpole. One of his most brilliant displays is preserved in the reported debate on a motion for an inquiry into the last ten years of that statesman's administration. The motion, tho carried in the House of Commons, was defeated of its object by a ministerial maneuver; but it sealed the ruin of the Walpole party, and yet affords a striking indication of the powers of this young and ardent and enlightened politician.

The Pelhams, who succeeded Walpole,

wishing to secure the cooperation of Pitt, attempted to get him brought into office; but a formidable obstacle stood in the way. The King was offended at Pitt for joining with the heir apparent to oppose the favorite minister and his Hanoverian politics; he refused to consent to his admission. The Pelhams resigned in consequence, but were shortly afterward reinstated, and brought Pitt along with them as vice-treasurer of Ireland in 1746. This post was soon converted into that of treasurer, and then exchanged for the place of privy-counselor, and paymaster-general of the forces. His conduct in this latter situation served to display the disinterested integrity of his nature; he disdained to retain any portion of the public money in his hands to profit by its interest, or by speculating with it in the funds, tho his predecessors had acted thus without scruple; he even refused the usual perquisites of his office, when they seemed unmerited by the duties of it. Such a manner of proceeding seemed to exmplify in practise the high principles which he had profest as an orator; it sanctioned and augmented the favor in which he had long stood over all the empire. With the king it was less successful. George II still viewed Pitt with a jealous eye, and Pitt was still inflexible in maintaining what he thought the true advantage of Britain against all the frowns of royalty and the intrigues of court. In the beginning of the seven years' war, when His Majesty returned from the continent, and presented the subsidiary treaties he had made with Hesse Cassel and Prussia for the defense of his beloved Hanover, Pitt did not hesitate to speak in Parliament against their ratification. He was, in consequence, dismist from office, and Mr. Legge, who has partaken in his fault, partook also in his punishment. This was in 1755.

Pitt was now again a private man, but surrounded with a blaze of reputation which few ministers would not have envied. The long and brave struggle he had made in defense of their privileges endeared him to the people; his virtue, proved alike in place and out of it, gave a new and more steady luster to the splendor which his high talents shed around him. In 1744 the Duchess of Marlborough had left him a legacy of £10,000, "upon account," as her testament exprest it, "of his merit in the noble defense he has made for the support of the laws of England, and to prevent the ruin of his country." Eleven years had now elapsed since the date of this splendid testimonial, nine of which had been spent in office, amid temptations such as have ruined the fame of many a patriot; yet still his popularity had continued to augment, and his late disfavor at court, by investing him with something of the grace of a martyr, had raised it to a higher pitch than ever. Men called him the Great Commoner; he was listened to by the nation as its guardian and father.

Happy in these circumstances of his public situation, Pitt was also happy in his domestic circle. In 1754 he had married Hester, only daughter of Richard Grenville, Esq., and of the Countess of Temple, a lady whose accomplishments, and graces, and affection formed a permanent solace to him throughout the remainder of his life. In a short time also he had reason to applaud the wisdom of his own anticipations and to pity the incapacity of the actual ministers. He spoke loudly against the policy of sending English money to defend Hanover by subsidies; he reprobated the idea of introducing Hanoverian soldiers to defend England. The course of events strongly seconded his reasoning; the beginning of the seven years' war was marked to Britain by nothing but disasters; the nation murmured; addresses and petitions called vehemently for a change, and the universal voice named Pitt as the man. His Majesty was again obliged to treat with this discarded servant. A new ministry was formed in 1756, in which Pitt took the post of Secretary of State, his friend Mr. Legge being Chancellor of the Exchequer. His Majesty's repugnance and difficulties are strongly marked by the fact that having a second time dismissed Pitt for his inflexible opposition to the Duke of Cumberland as general of the German war, he was again forced by the public opinion to recall him with the most ample concessions. Pitt resumed his place of Secretary on the 29th of June, 1757, and formed a cabinet according to his own choice. His personal influence, of course, was the predominating; he was unfettered by conflicting colleagues; even the king's prepossessions began to abate. Pitt, in their preliminary interview, had said to him, "Sire, give me your confidence and I will deserve it." His Majesty had answered, "Deserve it, and you shall have it." There was at least henceforth no visible discordance between them.

It was now that the genius of Pitt shone forth with unclouded splendor in the eyes of all Europe. Unconstrained in his movements, the vigor of his own mind seemed to pervade every department of the public service; its influence was soon felt in the remotest corners of the globe. He found the nation deprest and degraded; in three years he raised it to a height of greatness which it had never before attained. Devoting himself wholly to the duties of his office, entirely avoiding the pageantry of levees and public exhibitions, he bent himself with all his might to mature the plans he had formed for the national advantage and to discover fit instruments for realizing them. The extent of his information, the quickness of his understanding, enabled him at once to discover where the enemy was most assailable; his projects, magnificent as the mind that conceived them, were examined and provided for with the most scrupulous accuracy, and put in execution with an energy that insured success. The people were averse to any interference in the Continental war; Pitt objected less to the fact of interference than to the actual manner of it. Dismissing the Duke of Cumberland from the command of the army, to which the convention at Kloster-sieben had shown too well that he was unequal, he assisted Frederick of Prussia by subsidies, and gave the English troops to be led by Ferdinand of Brunswick. Some outcry was raised against him at first; it was thought he should have shaken off the interest of Hanover entirely. But he underwent these censures, persevered in his measures, and "conquered America in Germany," as he predicted. The French being occupied in these continental expeditions, and Frederick assisted by British gold to make head against them, their colonies and distant possessions were left ill guarded, and fell an easy prey to the vigorous attacks of the English. Before 1760 they had lost nearly all their foreign settlements; they were banished from Africa and Asia, and the Canadas had yielded to the heroism of Wolfe; the navy of France had scarcely an existence; her own coasts were continually insulted, and her people kept in constant terror of invasion. The talents and diligence of Pitt, the skill with which he administered the resources of Britain, had raised her to be the arbitress of Europe.

But all his triumphs abroad were insufficient to secure him against the vicissitudes of faction at home. In 1760 the king died, and the dependents of his successor, George III, began to look with eagerness for a change. It is hinted also that Pitt was not too agreeable to some of his colleagues. The great and uniform success of all his enterprises had exalted his reputation to a height which it was painful for a competitor to contemplate; and his habit of seeing every obstacle give way to the commanding effort of his will had strengthened in him that rigidness of manner, that imposing inflexibility of purpose, which his friends might dignify as the natural expression of a lofty and self-dependent mind, but which his enemies did not fail to brand with the name of arrogance or domineering ambition. The court sought a cause of quarrel with him, and one was not long occurring. By the accuracy of his intelligence he had discovered the existence of that family compact between the French and Spanish branches of the house of Bourbon, the secret influence of which had rendered abortive some recent attempts at making peace. With his characteristic decision, Pitt immediately moved for a declaration of war against Spain and a vigorous attack on her foreign possessions. He judged it better to surprize the enemy than be surprized by him; and the treachery of Spain seemed to authorize the omission of preliminary complaints and negotiations. The rest of the cabinet thought otherwise; the question was debated keenly; Pitt's opinion was overruled, and hints were given that his concurrence was no longer indispensable. The popularity of a young king, and the national desire for peace, warranted them in such proceedings; but it was against the minister's principle to incur responsibility where he had not the management. He resigned his office in October, 1761. The applause of all good men accompanied him in his retreat; he had the character of the most able and virtuous of statesmen. His private fortune was likewise increased by an annuity of £3,000, conferred on him at his resignation, to last during his life and that of his lady. The total inattention he had always manifested to his individual interests while managing the concerns of the public rendered this annuity a necessary gift. His lady was further honored with the rank of the peerage, conferred on her by the title of Baroness of Chatham.

Again reduced to a private station, Pitt attended chiefly to his duties in Parliament; and, without uniting himself to any party in the State, he kept a watchful eye over the public conduct of ministers, delivering his sentiments in the same fearless spirit which had hitherto distinguished all his public exhibitions. When the Peace of Paris, which his own exertions had done so much to bring about, was to be concluded in 1762, he exprest himself warmly against the terms of it —against the smallness of the benefit likely to result to England from the commanding attitude she had maintained throughout the latter years of the war. On the question of general warants, arising from the case of Wilkes, in 1764, he delivered an animated speech against the legality of such exertions of official prerogative, reminding his hearers "that an Englishman's house was his castle, defended not indeed by battlements and bulwarks, but by the impassable tho unseen barrier of law. It might be a straw-built shed, into which every wind of heaven might enter; but the king could not, the king dared not." That his popularity remained undiminished was evinced by a fact striking enough in itself, and more so as it regarded him. Sir William Pynsent, of Burton-Pynsent, in the County of Somerset, passed over his own family in order to bequeath an estate of £3,000 a year to this distinguished patriot. Already had the commencement of his political life been dignified by a similar tribute of approbation; it must have been doubly gratifying to find the same testimony still more unequivocally renewed when the busiest and most dangerous part of it was past.

Pitt was again to be a minister, but never so happy a one as he had been already. In 1766 the necessities of the government once more called him to a share in it; the formation of a new cabinet was intrusted to him, but the undertaking did not prosper in his hands. His brother-in-law and old associate, Lord Temple; his friend, the Marquis of Rockingham, could not enter in his views or act along with him, and the Great Commoner had offended many of his favorers by accepting a peerage. He was made Earl of Chatham and Baron of Burton-Pynsent prior to his entrance upon office. Of his ministry Mr. Burke has left us a curious and often-quoted description. The members of it were the most heterogeneous and discordant: the results they produced betrayed the feebleness of their union. Chatham resigned in two years, disgusted with the untowardness of his coadjutors, and tired of useless exertions to bend their clashing principles to a conformity with his own.

This was the last time he appeared in office. His strength and health were exhausted; years and excessive labor had increased the violence of his constitutional disorder; he wanted retirement and repose. His peerage had shut against him the habitual scene of his parliamentary exertions; he was not a constant attendant in the House of Lords; but when some great question called him forth from his retreat, the fire of his genius still shone with unabated brilliancy. The chief theme of his oratory from this period was the quarrel wth the American colonies, the interests and claims of which now began to occupy the principal share of the public attention. Chatham resisted the imposition of taxes on them; he warmly seconded the repeal of the Stamp Act. But when war had been undertaken—above all, when France had taken part in it—he was resolute in continuing in arms at whatever risk. The memorable scene in which he displayed his anxiety on this head is well known. On the 7th of April, 1778, the Duke of Richmond having moved an address to the King, in which the necessity of admitting the independence of America was broadly insinuated, Chatham deprecated such a consummation in the strongest terms. "I rejoice," said he, "that the grave has not closed upon me, that I am still alive to life up my voice against the dismemberment of this ancient and noble monarchy. Prest down as I am by the load of infirmity I am little able to assist my country in this most perilous conjuncture; but, my lords, while I have sense and memory I never will consent to tarnish the luster of this nation by an ignominious surrender of its rights and fairest possessions. Shall a people, so lately the terror of the world, now fall prostrate before the House of Bourbon? It is impossible! In God's name, if it is absolutely necessary to declare either for peace or war, and if peace can not be preserved with honor, why is not war commenced without hesitation? I am not, I confess, well informed of the resources of this kingdom, but I trust it has still sufficient to maintain its just rights tho I know them not. Any state, my lords, is better than despair. Let us at least make one effort; and if we must fall, let us fall like men." The duke replied, and Chatham made an eager effort to rise that he might speak further; but in vain, his voice was never more to be heard in that senate which it had so often dignified and delighted. He staggered, laid his hand upon his bosom, fainted, and was caught in the arms of the lords who sat near him and sprang to his assistance. They carried him into an adjoining room, and the House immediately adjourned. Medical assistance being procured, he was conveyed to his villa at Hayes, in Kent, where he lingered only till the following 11th of May, and then died, in the seventieth year of his age.

The circumstances of his death, combined with the general character of his life, render that event peculiarly impressive. News of it being conveyed to London by express, Colonel Barre reported the intelligence to Parliament, where it suspended all other business. The sense which the public entertained of their loss was manifested by the honors done to his memory. Party differences seemed to be forgot; all joined in voting that his debts should be paid by the nation, and that a yearly sum of £4,000 should be permanently added from the civil list to the title he had borne. He was buried in Westminster Abbey with all the pomp of a public funeral, and a piece of sculpture was afterward erected by way of monument, representing the last scene of his parliamentary life, and inscribed as the tribute of the King and Parliament to the Earl of Chatham.

The chief lineaments of Chatham's character may be gathered from the most meager chronicle of his actions. That he was a man of a splendid and impetuous genius—adapted for the duties of an orator by the vehemence of his feelings and the rich gifts of his intellect; for the duties of a statesman by his vastness of conception, his unwearied assiduity in ordering, his inflexible energy in execution—the highest and the humblest qualities that should combine to form a public man—may be learned from contemplating any portion of his public life. A survey of the whole will better show in how extraordinary a degree he possest these requisites, and how richly he adorned them all by a truly noble style of sentiment, a rigid adherence to the great principles of honor and generosity, and every manly virtue. And as his mind was singularly elevated, so had his fortune been singularly good. Few men that have acted so conspicuous a part have united so great a plurality of suffrages in their favor. The reason is that he founded no sect, was the father of no party, but of the party that love their country and labor for it; having thus been a genuine catholic in politics, his merits are admitted by all. Accordingly, the clamors that assailed him in life, the voice of obloquy and opposition, the memory of his failings, have long since died quite away, and Chatham is one in praise of whom the bitterest of partymen forgot their bitterness. He stands in the annals of Europe "an illustrious and venerable name," admired by countrymen and strangers, by all to whom loftiness of moral principle and greatness of talent are objects of regard.

"His private life," says Lord Chesterfield, "was stained by no vice, nor sullied by any meanness. All his sentiments were liberal and elevated. His ruling passion was an unbounded ambition, which, when supported by great abilities and crowned by great success, makes what the world calls a great man. He was haughty, imperious, impatient of contradiction, and overbearing—qualities which too often accompany, but always clog, great ones. He had manners and address; but one might discover through them too great a consciousness of his own superior talents. He was a most agreeable and lively companion in social life, and had such a versatility of wit that he could adapt it to all sorts of conversation. He had a most happy turn to poetry, but seldom indulged and seldom avowed it. His eloquence was of every kind, and he excelled in the argumentative as well as the declamatory way. But his invectives were terrible, and uttered with such energy of diction and such dignity of action and countenance, that he intimidated those who were most willing and best able to encounter him. Their arms fell out of their hands, and they struck under the ascendant which his genius gained over theirs.''

If Chatham's faculties had not been more worthily employed we might have regretted that he left so few memorials of them in a literary shape. Many of his speeches, under all the deformities of incorrect reporting, are full of beauty; and a volume of ''Letters'' to his nephew, published some years ago, may be read with a pleasure independent of their author. See ''Life of Chatham,'' in 3 volumes, and the public histories of the time.

ON THE ATHENIAN ORATORS

BY THOMAS BABINGTON MACAULAY

"To the famous orators repair,
Those ancient, whose resistless eloquence
Wielded at will that fierce democratic,
Shook the arsenal, and fulmined over Greece
To Macedon and Artaxerxes' throne."
—MILTON.

THE celebrity of the great classical writers is confined within no limits, except those which separate civilized from savage man. Their works are the common property of every polished nation. They have furnished subjects for the painter and models for the poet. In the minds of the educated classes throughout Europe their names are indissolubly associated with the endearing recollections of childhood—the old schoolroom, the dog-eared grammar, the first prize, the tears so often shed and so quickly dried. So great is the veneration with which they are regarded that even the editors and commentators who perform the lowest menial offices to their memory are considered, like the equerries and chamberlains of sovereign princes, as entitled to a high rank in the table of literary precedence. It is, therefore, somewhat singular that their productions should so rarely have been examined on just and philosophical principles of criticism.

STUDIES IN PROSE

The ancient writers themselves afford us but little assistance. When they particularize they are commonly trivial; when they would generalize they become indistinct. An exception must, indeed, be made in favor of Aristotle. Both in analysis and in combination that great man was without a rival. No philosopher has ever possest, in an equal degree, the talent either of separating established system into their primary elements, or of connecting detached phenomena in harmonious systems. He was the great fashioner of the intellectual chase; he changed its darkness into light, and its discord into order. He brought to literary researches the same vigor and amplitude of mind to which both physical and metaphysical science are so greatly indebted. His fundamental principles of criticism are excellent. To cite only a single instance: The doctrine which he established, that poetry is an imitative art when justly understood, is to the critic what the compass is to the navigator. With it he may venture upon the most extensive excursions. Without it he must creep cautiously along the coast, or lose himself in a trackless expanse, and trust, at best, to the guidance of an occasional star. It is a discovery which changes a caprice into a science.

The general propositions of Aristotle are valuable. But the merit of the superstructure bears no proportion to that of the foundation.

This is partly to be ascribed to the character of the philosopher, who, tho qualified to do all that could be done by the resolving and combining powers of the understanding, seems not to have possest much of sensibility or imagination. Partly, also, it may be attributed to the deficiency of materials. The great works of genius which then existed were not either sufficiently numerous or sufficiently varied to enable any man to form a perfect code of literature. To require that a critic should conceive classes of composition which had never existed, and then investigate their principles, would be as unreasonable as the demand of Nebuchadnezzar, who expected his magicians first to tell him his dream and then to interpret it.

With all his deficiencies, Aristotle was the most enlightened and profound critic of antiquity. Dionysius was far from possessing the same exquisite subtilty, or the same vast comprehension. But he had access to a much greater number of specimens, and he had devoted himself, as it appears, more exclusively to the study of elegant literature. His peculiar judgments are of more value than his general principles. He is only the historian of literature. Aristotle is its philosopher.

Quintilian applied to general literature the same principles by which he had been accustomed to judge of the declamations of his pupils. He looks for nothing but rhetoric, and rhetoric not of the highest order. He speaks coldly of the incomparable works of Æschylus. He admires beyond expression those inexhaustible mines of commonplaces, the plays of Euripides. He bestows a few vague words on the poetical character of Homer. He then proceeds to consider him merely as an orator. An orator Homer doubtless was, and a great orator. But surely nothing is more remarkable, in his admirable works than the art with which his oratorical powers are made subservient to the purposes of poetry. Nor can I think Quintilian a great critic in his own province. Just as are many of his remarks, beautiful as are many of his illustrations, we can perpetually detect in his thoughts that flavor which the soil of despotism generally communicates to all the fruits of genius. Eloquence was, in his time, little more than a condiment which served to stimulate in a despot the jaded appetite for panegyric, an amusement for the traveled nobles and the blue-stocking matrons of Rome. It is, therefore, with him rather a sport than a war; it is a contest of foils, not of swords. He appears to think more of the grace of the attitude than of the direction and vigor of the thrust. It must be acknowledged, in justice to Quintilian, that this is an error to which Cicero has too often given the sanction, both of his precept and of his example.

Longinus seems to have had great sensibility but little discrimination. He gives us eloquent sentences, but no principles. It was happily said that Montesquieu ought to have changed the name of his book from *L'Esprit des Lois* to *L'Esprit sur les Lois.* In the same manner the philosopher of Palmyra ought to have entitled his famous work, not "Longinus on the Sublime," but "The Sublimities of Longinus." The origin of the sublime is one of the most curious and interesting subjects of inquiry that can occupy the attention of a critic. In our own country it has been discust with great ability, and, I think, with very little success, by Burke and Dugald Stuart. Longinus dispenses himself from all investigations of this nature by telling his friend, Terentianus, that he already knows everything that can be said upon the question. It is to be regretted that Terentianus did not impart some of his knowledge to his instructor, for from Longinus we learn only that sublimity means height, or elevation. This name, so commodiously vague, is applied indifferently to the noble prayer of Ajax in the Iliad, and to a passage of Plato about the human body, as full of conceits as an ode of Cowley. Having no fixt standard, Longinus is right only by accident. He is rather a fancier than a critic.

Modern writers have been prevented by many causes from supplying the deficiencies of their classical predecessors. At the time

STUDIES IN PROSE

of the revival of literature no man could, without great and painful labor, acquire an accurate and elegant knowledge of the ancient languages. And, unfortunately, those grammatical and philological studies, without which it was impossible to understand the great works of Athenian and Roman genius, have a tendency to contract the views and deaden the sensibility of those who follow them with extreme assiduity. A powerful mind, which has been long employed in such studies, may be compared to the gigantic spirit in the Arabian tale, who was persuaded to contract himself to small dimensions in order to enter within the enchanted vessel, and, when his prison had been closed upon him, found himself unable to escape from the narrow boundaries to the measure of which he had reduced his stature. When the means have long been the objects of application they are naturally substituted for the end. It was said by Eugene of Savoy, that the greatest generals have commonly been those who have been at once raised to command, and introduced to the great operations of war, without being employed in the petty calculations and maneuvers which employ the time of an inferior officer. In literature the principle is equally sound. The great tactics of criticism will, in general, be best understood by those who have not had much practise in drilling syllables and particles.

I remember to have observed among the French Anas a ludicrous instance of this. A scholar, doubtless of great learning, recommends the study of some long Latin treatise, of which I now forget the name, on the religion, manners, government and language of the early Greeks. "For there," says he, "you will learn everything of importance that is contained in the Iliad and Odyssey, without the trouble of reading two such tedious books." Alas! it had not occurred to the poor gentleman that all the knowledge to which he attached so much value was useful only as it illustrated the great poems which he despised, and would be as worthless for any other purpose as the mythology of Caffragia or the vocabulary of Otaheite.

Of those scholars who have disdained to confine themselves to verbal criticism few have been successful. The ancient languages have, generally, a magical influence on their faculties. They were "fools called into a circle by Greek invocations." The Iliad and Æneid were to them not books, but curiosities, or, rather, relics. They no more amired those works for their merits than a good Catholic venerates the house of the Virgin at Loretto for its architecture. Whatever was classical was good. Homer was a great poet, and so was Calimachus. The epistles of Cicero were fine, and so were those of Phalaris. Even with respect to questions of evidence they fell into the same error. The authority of all narrations written in Greek or Latin was the same with them. It never crossed their minds that the lapse of five hundred years, or the distance of five hundred leagues, could affect the accuracy of a narration; that Livy could be a less veracious historian than Polybius, or that Plutarch could know less about the friends of Xenophon than Xenophon himself. Deceived by the distance of time, they seem to consider all the Classics as contemporaries; just as I have known people in England, deceived by the distance of place, take it for granted that all persons who live in India are neighbors, and ask an inhabitant of Bombay about the health of an acquaintance at Calcutta. It is to be hoped that no barbarian deluge will ever again pass over Europe. But, should such a calamity happen, it seems not improbable that some future Rollin or Gillies will compile a history of England from Miss Porter's "Scottish Chiefs," Miss Lee's "Recess," and Sir Nathaniel Wraxall's "Memoirs."

It is surely time that ancient literature should be examined in a different manner, without pedantical prepossessions, but with a just allowance at the same time for the difference of circumstances and manners. I am far from pretending to the knowledge or ability which such a task would require. I merely offer a collection of desultory remarks upon a most interesting portion of Greek literature.

It may be doubted whether any compositions which have ever been produced in the world are equally perfect in their kind with the great Athenian orations. Genius is subject to the same laws which regulate the production of cotton and molasses. The supply adjusts itself to the demand. The quantity may be diminished by restrictions and multiplied by bounties. The singular excellence to which eloquence attained at Athens is to be mainly attributed to the influence which it exerted there. In turbulent times, under a constitution purely democratic, among a people educated exactly to that point at which men are most susceptible of strong and sudden impressions, acute, but not sound reasoners, warm in their feelings, unfixt in their principles, and passionate admirers of fine composition, oratory received such encouragement as it has never since obtained.

The taste and knowledge of the Athenian people was a favorite object of the contemptuous derision of Samuel Johnson, a man who knew nothing of Greek literature beyond the common school-books, and who seems to have brought to what he had read scarcely more than the discernment of a common schoolboy. He used to assert, with that arrogant absurdity which, in spite of his great abilities and virtues, renders him, perhaps, the most ridiculous character in literary history, that Demosthenes spoke to a people of brutes—to a barbarous people; that there could have been no civilization before the invention of printing. Johnson was a keen but a very narrow-minded observer of mankind. He perpetually confounded their general nature with their particular circumstances. He knew London intimately. The sagacity of his remarks on its society is perfectly astonishing. But Fleet Street was the world to him. He saw that Londoners who did not read were profoundly ignorant; and he inferred that a Greek, who had few or no books, must have been as uninformed as one of Mr. Thrale's draymen.

There seems to be, on the contrary, every reason to believe that, in general intelligence, the Athenian populace far surpassed the lower orders of any community that has ever existed. It must be considered that to be a citizen was to be a legislator, a soldier, a judge— one upon whose voice might depend the fate of the wealthiest tributary state, of the most eminent public man. The lowest offices, both of agriculture and of trade, were, in common, performed by slaves. The commonwealth supplied its meanest members with the support of life, the opportunity of leisure, and the means of amusement. Books were indeed few; but they were excellent, and they were accurately known. It is not by turning over libraries, but by repeatedly perusing and intently contemplating a few great models, that the mind is best disciplined. A man of letters must now read much that he soon forgets, and much from which he learns nothing worthy to be remembered. The best works employ, in general, but a small portion of his time. Demosthenes is said to have transcribed six times the history of Thucydides. If he had been a young politician of the present age he might, in the same space of time, have skimmed innumerable newspapers and pamphlets. I do not condemn that desultory mode of study which the state of things in our day renders a matter of necessity. But I may be allowed to doubt whether the changes on which the admirers of modern institutions delight to dwell have improved our condition so much in reality as in apearance. Rumford, it is said, proposed to the Elector of Bavaria a scheme for feeding his soldiers at a much cheaper rate than formerly. His plan was simply to compel them to masticate their food thoroughly. A small quantity thus eaten would, according to that famous projector, afford more sustenance than a large meal hastily devoured. I do not know how Rumford's proposition was received; but to the mind, I believe, it will be found more nutritious to digest a page than to devour a volume.

Books, however, were the least part of the education of an Athenian citizen. Let us, for a moment, transport ourselves, in thought, to that glorious city. Let us imagine that we are entering its gates in the time of its power

STUDIES IN PROSE

and glory. A crowd is assembled round a portico. All are gazing with delight at the entablature, for Phidias is putting up the frieze. We turn into another street; a rhapsodist is reciting there; men, women, children are thronging round him; the tears are running down their cheeks, their eyes are fixt, their very breath is still, for he is telling how Priam fell at the feet of Achilles, and kissed those hands, the terrible, the murderous, which had slain so many of his sons. We enter the public place; there is a ring of youths, all leaning forward, with sparkling eyes and gestures of expectation. Socrates is pitted against the famous atheist from Ionia, and has just brought him to a contradiction in terms. But we are interrupted. The herald is crying, "Room for the Prytanes." The general assembly is to meet. The people are swarming in on every side. Proclamation is made: "Who wishes to speak?" There is a shout and a clapping of hands; Pericles is mounting the stand. Then for a play of Sophocles, and away to sup with Aspasia. I know of no modern university which has so excellent a system of education.

Knowledge thus acquired and opinions thus formed were, indeed, likely to be, in some respects, defective. Propositions which are advanced in discourse generally result from a partial view of the question, and can not be kept under examination long enough to be corrected. Men of great conversational powers almost universally practise a sort of lively sophistry and exaggeration, which deceives for the moment both themselves and their auditors. Thus we see doctrines which can not bear a close inspection triumph perpetually in drawing-rooms, in debating societies, and even in legislative or judicial assemblies. To the conversational eucation of the Athenians I am inclined to attribute the great looseness of reasoning which is remarkable in most of their scientific writings. Even the most illogical of modern writers would stand perfectly aghast at the puerile fallacies which seem to have deluded some of the greatest men of antiquity. Sir Thomas Lethbridge would stare at the political economy of Xenophon; and the author of "Soirées de Pétersbourg" would be ashamed of some of the metaphysical arguments of Plato. But the very circumstances which retarded the growth of science were peculiarly favorable to the cultivation of eloquence. From the early habit of taking a share in animated discussion the intelligent student would derive that readiness of resource, that copiousness of language, and that knowledge of the temper and understanding of an audience, which are far more valuable to an orator than the greatest logical powers.

Horace has prettily compared poems to those paintings of which the effect varies as

STUDIES IN PROSE

the spectator changes his stand. The same remark applies with at least equal justice to speeches. They must be read with the temper of those to whom they were addrest, or they must necessarily appear to offend against the laws of taste and reason, as the finest picture, seen in a light different from that for which it was designed, will appear fit only for a sign. This is perpetually forgotten by those who criticize oratory. Because they are reading at leisure, pausing at every line, reconsidering every argument, they forget that the hearers were hurried from point to point too rapidly to detect the fallacies through which they were conducted; that they had no time to disentangle sophisms, or to notice slight inaccuracies of expression; that elaborate excellence, either of reasoning or of language, would have been absolutely thrown away. To recur to the analogy of the sister art, these connoisseurs examine a panorama through a microscope, and quarrel with a scene-painter because he does not give to his work the exquisite finish of Gerard Dow.

Oratory is to be estimated on principles different from those which are applied to other productions. Truth is the object of philosophy and history. Truth is the object even of those works which are peculiarly called works of fiction, but which, in fact, bear the same relation to history which algebra bears to arithmetic. The merit of poetry, in its wildest forms, still consists in its truth—truth conveyed to the understanding, not directly by the words, but circuitously by means of imaginative associations, which serve as its conductors. The object of oratory alone is not truth, but persuasion. The admiration of the multitude does not make Moore a greater poet than Coleridge, or Beattie a greater philosopher than Berkeley. But the criterion of eloquence is different. A speaker who exhausts the whole philosophy of a question, who displays every grace of style, yet produces no effect on his audience, may be a great essayist, a great statesman, a great master of composition; but he is not an orator. If he miss the mark, it makes no difference whether he have taken aim too high or too low.

The effect of the great freedom of the press in England has been, in a great measure, to destroy this distinction, and to leave among us little of what I call oratory proper. Our legislators, our candidates on great occasions, even our advocates, address themselves less to the audience than to the reporters. They think less of the few hearers than of the innumerable readers. At Athens the case was different; there the only object of the speaker was immediate conviction and persuasion. He, therefore, who would justly appreciate the merit of the Grecian orators should place himself, as nearly as possible, in the situation of their auditors; he should divest himself of

STUDIES IN PROSE

his modern feelings and acquirements, and make the prejudices and interests of the Athenian citizen his own. He who studies their works in this spirit will find that many of those things which, to an English reader, appear to be blemishes—the frequent violation of those excellent rules of evidence by which our courts of law are regulated, the introduction of extraneous matter, the reference to considerations of political expediency in judicial investigations, the assertions without proof, the passionate entreaties, the furious invectives—are really proofs of the prudence and address of the speakers. He must not dwell maliciously on arguments or phrases, but acquiesce in his first impressions. It requires repeated perusal and reflection to decide rightly on any other portion of literature. But with respect to works of which the merit depends on their instantaneous effect the most hasty judgment is likely to be best.

The history of eloquence at Athens is remarkable. From a very early period great speakers had flourished there. Pisistratus and Themistocles are said to have owed much of their influence to their talents for debate. We learn with more certainty that Pericles was distinguished by extraordinary oratorical powers. The substance of some of his speeches is transmitted to us by Thucydides; and that excellent writer has doubtless faithfully reported the general line of his arguments.

But the manner, which in oratory is of at least as much consequence as the matter, was of no importance to his narration. It is evident that he has not attempted to preserve it. Throughout his work every speech on every subject, whatever may have been the character or the dialect of the speaker, is in exactly the same form. The grave King of Sparta, the furious demagog of Athens, the general encouraging his army, the captive supplicating for his life, all are represented as speakers in one unvaried style, a style moreover wholly unfit for oratorical purposes. His mode of reasoning is singularly elliptical, in reality most consecutive, yet in appearance often incoherent. His meaning, in itself sufficiently perplexing, is comprest into the fewest possible words. His great fondness for antithetical expression has not a little conduced to this effect. Every one must have observed how much more the sense is condensed in the verses of Pope and his imitators, who never ventured to continue the same clause from couplet to couplet, than in those of poets who allow themselves that license. Every artificial division which is strongly marked, and which frequently recurs, has the same tendency. The natural and perspicuous expression which spontaneously rises to the mind will often refuse to accommodate itself to such a form. It is necessary either to expand it into weakness, or to compress it into almost impenetrable density. The latter is generally the choice of an able man, and was assuredly the choice of Thucydides.

It is scarcely necessary to say that such speeches could never have been delivered. They are perhaps among the most difficult passages in the Greek language, and would probably have been scarcely more intelligible to an Athenian auditor than to a modern reader. Their obscurity was acknowledged by Cicero, who was as intimate with the literature and language of Greece as the most accomplished of its natives, and who seems to have held a respectable rank among the Greek authors. Their difficulty to a modern reader lies, not in the words, but in the reasoning. A dictionary is of far less use in studying them than a clear head and a close attention to the context. They are valuable to the scholar as displaying, beyond almost any other compositions, the powers of the finest of languages; they are valuable to the philosopher as illustrating the morals and manners of a most interesting age; they abound in just thought and energetic expression. But they do not enable us to form any accurate opinion on the merits of the early Greek orators.

Tho it can not be doubted that before the Persian wars Athens had produced eminent speakers, yet the period during which eloquence most flourished among her citizens was by no means that of her greatest power and glory. It commenced at the close of the Peloponnesian War. In fact, the steps by which Athenian oratory approached to its finished excellence seem to have been almost contemporaneous with those by which the Athenian character and the Athenian empire sank to degradation. At the time when the little commonwealth achieved those victories which twenty-five eventful centuries have left unequaled, eloquence was in its infancy. The deliverers of Greece became its plunderers and oppressors. Unmeasured exaction, atrocious vengeance, the madness of the multitude, the tyranny of the great, filled the Cyclades with tears, and blood, and mourning. The sword unpeopled whole islands in a day. The plow passed over the ruins of famous cities. The imperial republic sent forth her children by thousands to pine in the quarries of Syracuse, or to feed the vultures of Ægospotami. She was at length reduced by famine and slaughter to humble herself before her enemies, and to purchase existence by the sacrifice of her empire and her laws. During these disastrous and gloomy years oratory was advancing toward its highest excellence. And it was when the moral, the political, and the military charcter of the people was most utterly degraded, when the viceroy of a Macedonian sovereign gave law to Greece, that the courts of Athens witnessed the most splendid contest of eloquence the world had ever known.

STUDIES IN PROSE

The causes of this phenomenon it is not, I think, difficult to assign. The division of labor operates on the productions of the orator as it does on those of the mechanic. It was remarked by the ancients that the Pentathelete, who divided his attention between several exercises, tho he could not vie with a boxer in the use of the cestus, or with one who had confined his attention to running in the contest of the stadium, yet enjoyed far greater general vigor and health than either. It is the same with the mind. The superiority in technical skill is often more than compensated by the inferiority in general intelligence. And this is peculiarly the case in politics. States have always been best governed by men who have taken a wide view of public affairs, and who have rather a general acquaintance with many sciences than a perfect mastery of one. The union of the political and military departments in Greece contributed not a little to the splendor of its early history. After their separation more skilful generals and greater speakers appeared; but the breed of statesmen dwindled and became almost extinct. Themistocles or Pericles would have been no match for Demosthenes in the assembly, or for Iphicrates in the field. But surely they were incomparably better fitted than either for the supreme direction of affairs.

There is, indeed, a remarkable coincidence

between the progress of the art of war and that of the art of oratory among the Greeks. They both advanced to perfection by contemporaneous steps and from similar causes. The early speakers, like the early warriors of Greece, were merely a militia. It was found that in both employments practise and discipline gave superiority. Each pursuit therefore became first an art, and then a trade. In proportion as the professors of each became more expert in their particular craft, they became less respectable in their general character. Their skill had been obtained at too great expense to be employed only from disinterested views. Thus, the soldiers forgot that they were citizens, and the orators that they were statesmen. I know not to what Demosthenes and his famous contemporaries can be so justly compared as to those mercenary troops who, in their time, overran Greece; or those who, from similar causes, were some centuries ago the scourge of the Italian republics, perfectly acquainted with every part of their profession, irresistible in the field, powerful to defend or to destroy, but defending without love and destroying without hatred. We may despise the characters of these political *condottieri*, but it is impossible to examine the system of their tactics without being amazed at its perfection.

I had intended to proceed to this examination, and to consider separately the remains of

Lysias, or Æschines, or Demosthenes, and of Isocrates, who, tho strictly speaking he was rather a pamphleteer than an orator, deserves, on many accounts a place in such a disquisition. The length of my prolegomena and digressions compels me to postpone this part of the subject to another occasion. A magazine is certainly a delightful invention for a very idle or a very busy man. He is not compelled to complete his plan or to adhere to his subject. He may ramble as far as he is inclined, and stop as soon as he is tired. No one takes the trouble to recollect his contradictory opinions or his unredeemed pledges. He may be as superficial, as inconsistent, and as careless as he chooses. Magazines resemble those little angels who, according to the pretty rabbinical tradition, are generated every morning by the brook which rolls over the flowers of Paradise, whose life is a song, who warble till sunset, and then sink back without regret into nothingness. Such spirits have nothing to do with the detecting spear of Ithuriel or the victorious sword of Michael. It is enough for them to please and be forgotten.

LITERATURE*

BY JOHN HENRY CARDINAL NEWMAN

IN THE first place I observe that Literature, from the derivation of the word, implies writing, not speaking. This, however, arises from the circumstance of the copiousness, variety, and public circulation of the matters of which it consists. What is spoken can not outrun the range of the speaker's voice, and perishes in the uttering. When words are in demand to express a long course of thought, when they have to be conveyed to the ends of the earth, or perpetuated for the benefit of posterity, they must be written down—that is, reduced to the shape of literature. Still, properly speaking, the terms by which we denote this characteristic gift of man belong to its exhibition by means of the voice, not of handwriting. It addresses itself, in its primary idea, to the ear, not to the eye. We call it the power of speech, we call it language—that is, the use of the tongue; and, even when we write, we still keep in mind what was its original instrument, for we use freely such terms in our books as "saying," "speaking," "telling," "talking," "calling"; we use the terms "phraseology" and "dic-

*From "The Idea of a University," by kind permission of the publishers, Longmans, Green & Co., London.

tion," as if we were still addressing ourselves to the ear.

Now I insist on this, because it shows that speech, and therefore literature, which is its permanent record, is essentially a personal work. It is not some production or result, attained by the partnership of several persons, or by machinery, or by any natural process, but in its very idea it proceeds, and must proceed, from some one given individual. Two persons can not be the authors of the sounds which strike our ear; and, as they can not be speaking one and the same speech, neither can they be writing one and the same lecture or discourse, which must certainly belong to some one person or other, and is the expression of that one person's ideas and feelings— ideas and feelings personal to himself, tho others may have parallel and similar ones, proper to himself, in the same sense as his voice, his air, his countenance, his carriage, and his action are personal. In other words, literature expresses not objective truth, as it is called, but subjective; not things, but thoughts.

Now this doctrine will become clearer by considering another use of words, which does relate to objective truth, or to things; which relates to matters, not personal, not subjective to the individual, but which, even were there no individual man in the whole world to know them or to talk about them, would exist still.

Such objects become the matter of science, and words indeed are used to express them; but such words are rather symbols than language, and however many we use, and however we may perpetuate them by writing, we never could make any kind of literature out of them, or call them by that name. Such, for instance, would be Euclid's Elements; they relate to truths universal and eternal; they are not mere thoughts, but things: they exist in themselves, not by virtue of our understanding them, not in dependence upon our will, but in what is called the *nature* of things, or at least on conditions external to us. The words, then, in which they are set forth are not language, speech, literature, but rather as I have said, symbols. And, as a proof if it, you will recollect that it is possible—nay, usual—to set forth the propositions of Euclid in algebraical notation, which, as all would admit, has nothing to do with literature. What is true of mathematics is true also of every study, so far forth as it is scientific; it makes use of words as the mere vehicle of things, and is thereby withdrawn from the province of literature. Thus, metaphysics, ethics, law, political economy, chemistry, theology, cease to be literature in the same degree as they are capable of a severe scientific treatment. And hence it is that Aristotle's works on the one hand, tho at first sight literature, approach in character—at least a great number of them—to mere science; for even tho the things which he treats of and exhibits may not always be real and true, yet he treats them as if they were, not as if they were the thoughts of his own mind; that is, he treats them scientifically. On the other hand, law or natural history has before now been treated by an author with so much of coloring derived from his own mind as to become a sort of literature. This is especially seen in the instance of theology when it takes the shape of pulpit eloquence. It is seen, too, in historical composition, which becomes a mere specimen of chronology, or a chronicle, when divested of the philosophy, the skill, or the party and personal feelings of the particular writer. Science, then, has to do with things; literature with thoughts; science is universal, literature is personal; science uses words merely as symbols, but literature uses language in its full compass, as including phraseology, idiom, style, composition, rhythm, eloquence, and whatever other properties are included in it.

Let us, then, put aside the scientific use of words when we are to speak of language and literature. Literature is the personal use or exercise of language. That this is so is further proved from the fact that one author uses it so differently from another. Language itself in its very origination would seem to be traceable to individuals. Their peculiarities have given it its character. We are often able, in fact, to trace particular phrases or idioms to individuals; we know the history of their rise. Slang surely, as it is called, comes of and breathes of the personal. The connection between the force of words in particular languages and the habits and sentiments of the nations speaking them has often been pointed out. And, while the many use language as they find it, the man of genius uses it, indeed, but subjects it withal to his own purposes, and molds it according to his own peculiarities. The throng and succession of ideas, thoughts, feelings, imaginations, aspirations, which pass within him, the abstractions, the juxtapositions, the comparisons, the discriminations, the conceptions, which are so original in him; his views of external things, his judgments upon life, manners and history, the exercises of his wit, of his humor, of his depth, of his sagacity, all these innumerable and incessant creations, the very pulsation and throbbing of his intellect, does he image forth, to all does he give utterance, in a corresponding language, which is as multiform as this inward mental action itself and analogous to it, the faithful expression of his intense personality, attending on his own inward world of thought as its very shadow; so that we might as well say that one man's shadow is another's as that the style of a really gifted mind can belong to any but himself. It follows him about *as* a shadow. His thought and feeling are personal, and so his language is personal.

Thought and speech are inseparable from each other. Matter and expression are parts of one; style is a thinking out into language. This is what I have been laying down, and this is literature; not *things,* not the verbal symbols of things; not, on the other hand, mere *words,* but thoughts exprest in language. Call to mind, gentlemen, the meaning of the Greek word which expresses this special prerogative of man over the feeble intelligence of the inferior animals. It is called *logos.* What does *logos* mean? It stands both for *reason* and for *speech*, and it is difficult to say which it means more properly. It means both at once. Why? Because really they can not be divided, because they are in a true sense one. When we can separate light and illumination, life and motion, the convex and the concave of a curve, then it will be possible for thought to tread speech under foot and to hope to do without it; then will it be conceivable that the vigorous and fertile intellect should renounce its own double, its instrument of expression, and the channel of its speculations and emotions.

Critics should consider this view of the subject before they lay down such canons of taste as the writer whose pages I have quoted. Such men as he is consider fine writing to be an *addition from without* to the matter treated of—a sort of ornament superinduced, or a luxury indulged in, by those who have time and inclination for such vanities. They speak as if *one* man could do the thought and *another* the style. We read in Persian travels of the way in which young gentlemen go to work in the East, when they would engage in correspondence with those who inspire them with hope or fear. They can not write one sentence themselves; so they betake themselves to the professional letter-writer. They confide to him the object they have in view. They have a point to gain from a superior, a favor to ask, an evil to deprecate; they have to approach a man in power, or to make court to some beautiful lady. The professional man manufactures words for them as they are wanted, as a stationer sells them paper, or a schoolmaster might cut their pens. Thoughts and words are, in their conception, two things, and thus there is a division of labor. The man of thought comes to the man of words; and the man of words, duly instructed in the thought, dips the pen of desire into the ink of devotedness, and proceeds to spread it over the page of desolation. Then the nightingale of affection is heard to warble to the rose of loveliness, while the breeze of anxiety plays around the brow of expectation. This is what the Easterns are said to consider fine writing; and it seems pretty much the idea of the school of critics to whom I have been referring.

STUDIES IN PROSE

We have an instance in literary history of this very proceeding nearer home, in a great university, in the latter years of the last century. I have referred to it before now in a public lecture elsewhere; but it is too much in point here to be omitted. A learned Arabic scholar had to deliver a set of lectures before its doctors and professors on an historical subject in which his reading had lain. A linguist is conversant with science rather than with literature; but this gentleman felt that his lectures must not be without a style. Being of the opinion of the Orientals, with whose writings he was familiar, he determined to create a style. He took the step of engaging a person, at a price, to turn the matter which he had got together into ornamental English. Observe, he did not wish for mere grammatical English, but for an elaborate, pretentious style. An artist was found in the person of a county curate, and the job was carried out. His lectures remain to this day in their own place in the protracted series of annual discourses to which they belong, distinguished amid a number of heavyish compositions by the rhetorical and ambitious diction for which he went into the market. This learned divine, indeed, and the author I have quoted, differ from each other in the estimate they respectively form of literary composition; but they agree together in this—in considering such composition a trick and a trade; they put it on a par with the gold plate and the flowers and the music of a banquet, which do not make the viands better but the entertainment more pleasurable, as if language were the hired servant, the mere mistress of the reason, and not the lawful wife in her own house.

But can they really think that Homer, or Pindar, or Shakespeare, or Dryden, or Walter Scott were accustomed to aim at diction for its own sake, instead of being inspired with their subject, and pouring forth beautiful words because they had beautiful thoughts? This is surely too great a paradox to be borne. Rather, it is the fire within the author's breast which overflows in the torrent of his burning, irresistible eloquence; it is the poetry of his inner soul, which relieves itself in the ode or the elegy; and his mental attitude and bearing, the beauty of his moral countenance, the force and keenness of his logic, are imaged in the tenderness, or energy, or richness of his language. Nay, according to the well-known line, "Facit indignatio *versus*"; not the words alone, but even the rhythm, the metre, the verse, will be the contemporaneous offspring of the emotion or imagination which possesses him. "Poeta nascitur, non fit," says the proverb; and this is in numerous instances true of his poems as well as of himself. They are born, not framed; they are a strain rather than a composition; and their perfection is the monument, not so much of his

STUDIES IN PROSE

skill as of his power. And this is true of prose as well as of verse in its degree. Who will not recognize in the vision of Mirza a delicacy and beauty of style which is very difficult to describe, but which is felt to be in exact correspondence to the ideas of which it is the expression?

And, since the thoughts and reasonings of an author have, as I have said, a personal character, no wonder that his style is not only the image of his subject, but of his mind. That pomp of language, that full and tuneful diction, that felicitousness in the choice and exquisiteness in the collocation of words, which to prosaic writers seem artificial, is nothing else but the mere habit and way of a lofty intellect. Aristotle, in his sketch of the magnanimous man, tells us that his voice is deep, his emotions slow, and his stature commanding. In like manner the elocution of a great intellect is great. His language expresses, not only his great thoughts, but his brief self. Certainly he might use fewer words than he uses; but he fertilizes his simplest ideas, and germinates into a multitude of details, and prolongs the march of his sentences, and sweeps round to the full diapason of his harmony, as if rejoicing in his own vigor and richness of resource. I say, a narrow critic will call it verbiage, when really it is a sort of fulness of heart, parallel to that which makes the merry boy whistle as he walks, or the strong man, like the smith in the novel, flourish his club when there is no one to fight with.

Shakespeare furnishes us with frequent instances of this peculiarity, and all so beautiful that it is difficult to select for quotation. For instance, in "Macbeth":

"Canst thou not minister to a mind diseased,
Pluck from the memory a rooted sorrow,
Raze out the written troubles of the brain,
And, with some sweet oblivious antidote,
Cleanse the foul bosom of that perilous stuff,
Which weighs upon the heart?"

Here a simple idea, by a process which belongs to the orator rather than to the poet, but still comes from the native vigor of genius, is expanded into a many-membered period.

The following, from "Hamlet," is of the same kind:

" 'Tis not alone my inky cloak, good mother
Nor customary suits of solemn black,
Nor windy suspiration of forced breath,
No, nor the fruitful river in the eye,
Nor the dejected haviour of the visage,
Together with all forms, modes, shows of grief,
That can denote me truly."

Now, if such declamation, for declamation it is, however noble, be allowable in a poet, whose genius is so far removed from pompousness or pretense, much more is it allowable in an orator, whose very province it is to put forth words to the best advantage he can.

STUDIES IN PROSE

Cicero has nothing more redundant in any part of his writings than these passages from Shakespeare. No lover then, at least, of Shakespeare may fairly accuse Cicero of gorgeousness of phraseology or diffuseness of style. Nor will any sound critic be tempted to do so. As a certain unaffected neatness and propriety and grace of diction may be required of any author who lays claim to be a classic, for the same reason that a certain attention to dress is expected of every gentleman, so to Cicero may be allowed the privilege of the "os magna sonaturum," of which the ancient critic speaks. His copious, majestic, musical flow of language, even if sometimes beyond what the subject-matter demands, is never out of keeping with the occasion or with the speaker. It is the expression of lofty sentiments in lofty sentences, the "mens magna in corpore magno." It is the development of the inner man. Cicero vividly realized the *status* of a Roman, senator and statesman, and the "pride of place" of Rome, in all the grace and grandeur which attached to her; and he imbibed, and became what he admired. As the exploits of Scipio or Pompey are the expression of this greatness in deed, so the language of Cicero is the expression of it in word. And, as the acts of the Roman ruler or soldier represent to us, in a manner special to themselves, the characteristic magnanimity of the lords of the earth, so do the speeches or treatises of her accomplished orator bring it home to our imaginations as no other writing could do. Neither Livy, nor Tacitus, nor Terence, nor Seneca, nor Pliny, nor Quintilian, is an adequate spokesman for the Imperial City. They write Latin; Cicero writes Roman.

"You will say that Cicero's language is undeniably studied, but that Shakespeare's is as undeniably natural and spontaneous; and that is what is meant when the Classics are accused of being mere artists of words. Here we are introduced to a further large question, which gives me the opportunity of anticipating a misapprehension of my meaning. I observe, then, that not only is that lavish richness of style which I have noticed in Shakespeare justifiable on the principles which I have been laying down, but, what is less easy to receive, even elaborateness in composition is no mark of trick or artifice in an author. Undoubtedly, the works of the classics, particularly the Latin, *are* elaborate; they have cost a great deal of time, care and trouble. They have had many rough copies, I grant it. I grant also that there are writers of name, ancient and modern, who really are guilty of the absurdity of making sentences, as the very end of their literary labor. Such was Isocrates; such were some of the sophists. They were set on words, to the neglect of thoughts or things; I can not defend them. If I must give an English instance of this fault, much as I love and revere the personal character and intellectual vigor of Doctor Johnson, I can not deny that his style often outruns the sense and the occasion, and is wanting in that simplicity which is the attribute of genius. Still, granting all this, I can not grant, notwithstanding, that genius never need take pains, that genius may not improve by practise, that it never incurs failures, and succeeds the second time, that it never finishes off at leisure what it has thrown off in the outline at a stroke.

Take the instance of the painter or the sculptor; he has a conception in his mind which he wishes to represent in the medium of his art—the Madonna and the Child, or Innocence, or Fortitude, or some historical character or event. Do you mean to say he does not study his subject? Does he not make sketches? Does he not even call them "studies?" Does he not call his workroom a *studio?* Is he not ever designing, rejecting, adopting, correcting, perfecting? Are not the first attempts of Michelangelo and Raffael extant in the case of some of their most celebrated compositions? Will any one say that Apollo Belvidere is not a conception patiently elaborated into its proper perfection? These departments of taste are, according to the received notions of the world, the very province of genius, and yet we call them *arts;* they are the "Fine Arts." Why may not that be true of literary composition which is true of painting, sculpture, architecture and music? Why may not language be wrought as well as the clay of the modeler? Why may not words be worked up as well as colors? Why should not skill in diction be simply subservient and instrumental to the great prototypal ideas which are the contemplation of a Plato or a Vergil? Our greatest poet tells us,

> "The poet's eye, in a fine frenzy rolling,
> Doth glance from heaven to earth, from earth to heaven,
> And, as imagination bodies forth
> The forms of things unknown, the poet's pen
> Turns them to shapes, and gives to airy nothing
> A local habitation and a name."

Now, is it wonderful that that pen of his should sometimes be at fault for a while—that it should pause, write, erase, rewrite, amend, complete, before he satisfies himself that his language has done justice to the conceptions which his mind's eye contemplated?

In this point of view, doubtless, many or most writers are elaborate; and those certainly not the least whose style is furthest removed from ornament, being simple and natural, or vehement, or severely business-like and practical. Who so energetic and manly as Demosthenes? Yet he is said to have transcribed Thucydides many times over in the formation of his style. Who so gracefully natural as Herodotus? Yet his very dialect

STUDIES IN PROSE

is not his own, but chosen for the sake of perfection of his narrative. Who exhibits such happy negligence as our own Addison? Yet artistic fastidiousness was so notorious in his instance that the report has got abroad, truly or not, that he was too late in his issue of an important state paper from his habit of revision and recomposition. Such great authors were working by a model which was before the eyes of their intellect, and they were laboring to say what they had to say in such a way as would most exactly and suitably express it. It is not wonderful that other authors, whose style is not simple, should be instances of a similar literary diligence. Vergil wished his Æneid to be burned, elaborate as is its composition, because he felt it needed more labor still, in order to make it perfect. The historian Gibbon, in the last century, is another instance in point. You must not suppose I am going to recommend his style for imitation, any more than his principles; but I refer to him as the example of a writer feeling the task which lay before him, feeling that he had to bring out into words for the comprehension of his readers a great and complicated scene, and wishing that those words should be adequate to his undertaking. I think he wrote the first chapter of his History three times over. It was not that he corrected or improved the first copy; but he put his first essay, and then his second, aside; he recast his matter, till he had hit the precise exhibition of it which he thought demanded by his subject.

Now in all these instances I wish you to observe that what I have admitted about literary workmanship differs from the doctrine which I am opposing in this—that the mere dealer in words cares little or nothing for the subject which he is embellishing, but can paint and gild anything whatever to order; whereas the artist, whom I am acknowledging, has his great or rich visions before him, and his only aim is to bring out what he thinks or what he feels in a way adequate to the thing spoken of, and appropriate to the speaker.

The illustration which I have been borrowing from the Fine Arts will enable me to go a step further. I have been showing the connection of the thought with the language in literary composition, and in doing so I have exposed the unphilosophical notion that the language was an extra which could be dispensed with, and provided to order according to the demand. But I have not yet brought out what immediately follows from this, and which was the second point which I had to show, viz., that to be capable of easy translation is no test of the excellence of a composition. If I must say what I think, I should lay down, with little hesitation, that the truth was almost the reverse of this doctrine. Nor are many words required to show it. Such a doctrine, as is contained in the passage of the author whom I quoted when I began, goes upon the assumption that one language is just like another language; that every language has all the ideas, turns of thought, delicacies of expression, figures, associations, abstractions, points of view, which every other language has. Now, as far as regards Science, it is true that all languages are pretty much alike for the purposes of Science; but even in this respect some are more suitable than others, which have to coin words, or to borrow them, in order to express scientific ideas. But if languages are not all equally adapted even to furnish symbols for those universal and eternal truths in which Science consists, how can they reasonably be expected to be all equally rich, equally forcible, equally musical, equally exact, equally happy in expressing the idiosyncratic peculiarities of thought of some original and fertile mind, who has availed himself of one of them? A great author takes his native language, masters it, partly throws himself into it, partly molds and adapts it, and pours out his multitude of ideas through the variously ramified and delicately minute channels of expression which he has found or framed. Does it follow that this, his personal presence (as it may be called), can forthwith be transferred to every other language under the sun? Then may we reasonably maintain that Beethoven's *piano* music is not really beautiful because it can not be played on the hurdy-gurdy. Were not this astonishing doctrine maintained by persons far superior to the writer whom I have selected for animadversion, I should find it difficult to be patient under a gratuitous extravagance. It seems that a really great author must admit of translation, and that we have a test of his excellence when he reads to advantage in a foreign language as well as in his own. Then Shakespeare *is* a genius because he can be translated into German, and *not* a genius because he can not be translated into French. Then the multiplication table is the most gifted of all conceivable composition, because it loses nothing by translation, and can hardly be said to belong to any one language whatever. Whereas I should rather have conceived that, in proportion as ideas are novel or recondite, they would be difficult to put into words, and that they very fact of their having insinuated themselves into one language would diminish the chance of that happy incident being repeated in another. In the language of savages you can hardly express any idea or act of the intellect at all. Is the tongue of the Hottentot or Eskimo to be made the measure of the genius of Plato, Pindar, Tacitus, St. Jerome, Dante, or Cervantes?

Let us recur, I say, to the illustration of the Fine Arts. I suppose you can express ideas in painting which you can not express in sculpture; and the more an artist is of a painter, the less he is likely to be of a sculptor. The more he commits his genius to the methods and conditions of his own art, the less he will be able to throw himself into the circumstances of another. Is the genius of Fra Angelico, of Francia, or of Raffael disparaged by the fact that he was able to do that in colors which no man that ever lived, which no angel, could achieve in wood? Each of the fine arts has its own subject-matter. From the nature of the case you can do in one what you can not do in another; you can do in painting what you can not do in carving; you can do in oils what you can not do in fresco; you can do in marble what you can not do in ivory; you can do in wax what you can not do in bronze. Then, I repeat, applying this to the case of languages, why should not genius be able to do in Greek what it can not do in Latin? And why are its Greek and Latin works defective because they will not turn into English? That genius, of which we are speaking, did not make English; it did not make all languages, present, past and future; it did not make the laws of *any* language. Why is it to be judged of by that in which it had no part, over which it has no control?

And now we are naturally brought on to our third point, which is on the characteristics of Holy Scripture as compared with profane literature. Hitherto we have been concerned with the doctrine of these writers, viz., that style is an *extra,* that it is a mere artifice, and that hence it can not be translated. Now we come to their fact, viz., that Scripture has no such artificial style, and that Scripture can easily be translated. Surely their fact is as untenable as their doctrine.

Scripture easy of translation! Then why have there been so few good translators? Why is it that there has been such great difficulty in combining the two necessary qualities, fidelity to the original and purity in the adopted vernacular? Why is it that the authorized versions of the Church are often so inferior to the original as compositions, except that the Church is bound, above all things, to see that the version is doctrinally correct, and in a difficult problem is obliged to put up with defects in what is of secondary importance, provided she secure what is of first? If it were so easy to transfer the beauty of the original to the copy, she would not have been content with her received version in various languages which could be named.

And then, in the next place, Scripture not elaborate! Scripture not ornamented in diction and musical in cadence! Why, consider the Epistle to the Hebrews. Where is there in the classics any composition more carefully, more artificially written? Consider the Book of Job: Is it not a sacred drama, as artistic, as perfect, as any Greek tragedy of Sophocles or Euripides? Consider the Psalter: Are there no ornaments, no rhythm, no studied cadences, no responsive members, in that divinely beautiful book? And is it not hard to understand? Is not Saint Paul hard to understand? Who can say that these are popular compositions? Who can say that they are level at first reading with the understandings of the multitude?

That there are portions indeed of the inspired volume more simple both in style and in meaning, and that these are the more sacred and sublime passages, as, for instance, parts of the Gospels, I grant at once; but this does not militate against the doctrine I have been laying down. Recollect, gentlemen, my distinction when I began. I have said literature is one thing, and that science is another; that literature has to do with ideas, and science with realities; that literature is of a personal character, that science treats of what is universal and eternal. In proportion, then, as Scripture excludes the personal coloring of its writers, and rises into the region of pure and mere inspiration, when it ceases in any sense to be the writing of man, Saint Paul or Saint John, of Moses or Isaiah, then it comes to belong to science, not literature. Then it conveys the things of heaven, unseen verities, divine manifestations, and them alone—not the ideas, the feelings, the aspirations, of its human instruments, who, for all that they were inspired and infallible, did not cease to be men. Saint Paul's epistles, then, I consider to be literature in a real and true sense, *as* personal, *as* rich in reflection and emotion, as Demosthenes or Euripides; and, without ceasing to be revelations of objective truth, they are expressions of the subjective, notwithstanding. On the other hand, portions of the Gospels, of the book of Genesis, and other passages of the Sacred Volume, are of the nature of science. Such is the beginning of Saint John's Gospel, which we read at the end of Mass. Such is the Creed. I mean, passages such as these are the mere enunciation of eternal things, without (so to say) the medium of any human mind transmitting them to us. The words used have the grandeur, the majesty, the calm, unimpassioned beauty of science; they are in no sense literature, they are in no sense personal; and therefore they are easy to apprehend, and easy to translate.

Did time admit I could show you parallel instances of what I am speaking of in the classics inferior to the inspired word in proportion as the subject-matter of the classical authors is immensely inferior to the subjects treated of in Scripture, but parallel, inasmuch as the classical author or speaker ceases for the moment to have to do with literature, as speaking of things objectively, and rises to the serene sublimity of science. But I should be carried too far if I began.

I shall then merely sum up what I have said,

and come to a conclusion. Reverting, then, to my original question, what is the meaning of letters, as contained, gentlemen, in the designation of your faculty, I have answered, that by letters or literature is meant the expression of thought in language, where by "thought" I mean the ideas, feelings, views, reasonings, and other operations of the human mind. And the art of letters is the method by which a speaker or writer brings out in words, worthy of his subject, and sufficient for his audience or readers, the thoughts which impress him. Literature, then, is of a personal character; it consists in the enunciations and teachings of those who have a right to speak as representatives of their kind, and in those words their brethren find an interpretation of their own sentiments, a record of their own experience, and a suggestion for their own judgments. A great author, gentlemen, is not one who merely has a *copia verborum,* whether in prose or verse, and can, as it were, turn on at his will any number of splendid phrases and swelling sentences; but he is one who has something to say and knows how to say it. I do not claim for him, as such, any great depth of thought, or breadth of view, or philosophy, or sagacity, or knowledge of human nature, or experience of human life, tho these additional gifts he may have, and the more he has of them the greater he is; but I ascribe to him, as his characteristic gift, in a large sense the faculty of expression. He is master of the twofold Logos, the thought and the word, distinct, but inseparable from each other. He may, if so be, elaborate his compositions, or he may pour out his improvisations, but in either case he has but one aim, which he keeps steadily before him, and is conscientious and single-minded in fulfilling. That aim is to give forth what he has within him; and from his very earnestness it comes to pass that, whatever be the splendor of his diction or the harmony of his periods, he has with him the charm of an incommunicable simplicity. Whatever be his subject, high or low, he treats it suitably and for its own sake. If he is a poet, "nil molitur *inepte.*" If he is an orator, then, too, he speaks, not only "distincte" and "splendide," but also *"apte."* His page is the lucid mirror of his mind and life—

> "Quo fit, ut omnis
> Votiva pateat veluti descripta tabella
> Vita senis."

He writes passionately, because he feels keenly; forcibly, because he conceives vividly. He sees too clearly to be vague; he is too serious to be otiose; he can analyze his subject, and therefore he is rich; he embraces it as a whole and in its parts, and therefore he is consistent; he has a firm hold of it, and therefore he is luminous. When his imagination wells up, it overflows in ornament; when his heart is touched, it thrills along his verse. He always has the right word for the right idea, and never a word too much. If he is brief, it is because few words suffice; when he is lavish of them, still each word has its mark, and aids, not embarrasses, the vigorous march of his elocution. He expresses what all feel, but all can not say; and his sayings pass into proverbs among his people, and his phrases become household words and idioms of their daily speech, which is tessellated with the rich fragments of his language, as we see in foreign lands the marbles of Roman grandeur worked into the walls and pavements of modern palaces.

Such preeminently is Shakespeare among ourselves; such preeminently Vergil among the Latins; such in their degree are all those writers who in every nation go by the name of Classics. To particular nations they are necessarily attached from the circumstances of the variety of tongues and the peculiarities of each; but so far they have a catholic and ecumenical character, that what they express is common to the whole race of man, and they alone are able to express it.

If then the power of speech is a gift as great as any that can be named, if the origin of language is by many philosophers even considered to be nothing short of divine, if by means of words the secrets of the heart are brought to light, pain of soul is relieved, hidden grief is carried off, sympathy conveyed, counsel imparted, experience recorded and wisdom perpetuated; if by great authors the many are drawn up into unity, national character is fixt, a people speaks, the past and the future, the east and the west are brought into communication with each other; if such men are, in a word, the spokesmen and prophets of the human family, it will not answer to make light of literature or to neglect its study; rather we may be sure that, in proportion as we master it in whatever language, and imbibe its spirit, we shall ourselves become in our own measure the ministers of like benefits to others, be they many or few, be they in the obscurer or the more distinguished walks of life, who are united to us by social ties, and are within the sphere of our personal influence.

SPEECH AND THOUGHT

BY RUDOLF HERMANN LOTZE

(From "Microcosmus")*

In whatever may consist that state of excitation into which the nerves of sense are brought by external stimuli, it at any rate presents a definite amount of some physical motion of masses that by the law of persistence can not cease of itself, but must either be stopt by some definite resistance or reduced to zero by distribution over the environment. If the organs of sense are designed to be to us a medium of knowledge of the outer world, it is necessary, in order to our receiving this unadulterated, that the tremor produced by the impression of one moment should rapidly be so far mitigated as not to counteract the impression of the next moment or blend with it as an adulterative element. So long as the physical stimuli by which the senses are acted on are but inconsiderable amounts of motion, this perpetual effacement of their effects may be accomplished partly within the organ of sense through the uninterrupted processes of the transformation of matter, partly through the

---

*From "Microcosmus," by kind permission of the publishers, T. & T. Clark, Edinburgh.

generation of the sensation itself. For even sensation, as a newly manifested internal phenomenon of the soul, which as a substance stands in a mechanical relation of reciprocal action with the elements of the body, can not merely arise on occasion of nerve-stimulation; part of the latter must be utilized in its production. The stimuli of light and sound constantly acting on us keep within these limits of intensity, and we are not aware of any special corrective agency by which their influence require to be adjusted. If, on the other hand, external impressions reach a painful degree of strength, we must expect to find a corresponding provision of means for their removal. Now, as it is the office of the nerve-filaments to transmit to the brain the stimulations received at their extremities, it is not to be supposed that this provision can consist in any sudden hindrance to transmission, or in any considerably increased distribution of the stimulation in all directions. Both are unfavorable to the natural function of the sensory nerve, and we may look on it as universally characteristic of the organization that it meets threatening disturbances not with new and unusual means, but with means of a type that has already appeared in the healthy condition. So long, then, as the intensity of the stimulus does not directly injure the nerve, and thereby, of course, preclude the further effects of a too violent impression, we assume that the excitation is transmitted to the central organs and dissipated by there producing a larger proportion of after-affects, the fainter traces of which may be discerned even in the ordinary degrees of stimulation.

Three roads are open for the further extension of the stimulation in the brain; for the sensory nerve finds there: (1) other sensory nerves; (2) sympathetic nerves; (3) motor nerves. The transference of its excitation to other sensory nerves, consequently the production of an accompanying sensation in other than the actually stimulated parts, must be confined with a narrow range if the purpose of sentience, to bring about somehow a knowledge of the outer world, is not to be too much restricted. As a matter of fact, the strongest stimulation of one organ of sense does not produce any distinct stimulation of another; excess of light produces no sensation of sound; a loud sound no sensation of smell. Only the general sense shares in the disturbance through the change effected in its states. A transference of the stimulation to the vegetative filaments of the sympathetic system would be more advantageous, because among the manifold functions of these nerves there are many that without any detrimental effect on life can be for the moment increased in amount, and by which, as well as by many alterations in the process of material transformation due to them, the disturbance of the organism can be harmlessly carried off. The phenomena of fever offer an example of transference of excitation in this direction. But in the natural course of life the sensations are specially designed to serve as incitements to movements by which the soul somehow subjects perceived objects to its elaborating processes. So many reasons render necessary the close connection of sensory with motor nerves and the excitation of movements by the direct action of the former, that we can not wonder if even painful disturbances are for the most part counteracted in this way—always kept open for the purposes of healthy life—viz., by a communication to motor nerves, consequently by means of the production of motion.

Hence it is that we find all violent pains in the living body, powerful irritants even in decapitated animals, call forth movements at first in the immediately affected parts, as the impression becomes stronger throughout the whole body. Sometimes there comes to be a changeful succession of these, a tremulous agitation of the whole body—sometimes, where a strong effort at patient endurance is made, a rigid, persistent, exceedingly violent contraction of a single group of muscles is brought about, in order that in the surplus energy here expended the internal stimulation may have an outlet. So the sufferer grinds his teeth or clenches fists, or straightens his back and stretches out his aimlessly stiffened leg. At last the persistent or increasing irritation withdraws these movements from the influence of the will and exhausts itself in incessant spasmodic attacks. Mental agitations from within act upon the nerves in the same fashion as the sense-impressions coming from without do here. In view of the reciprocal action between body and soul, we can not look upon these two processes as running their course exclusively within the latter and requiring special causes to make them assume a corporeal form; from the first they are a certain quantum of effective motion, whose impression on the body, instead of needing to be brought to bear by special means, must by special means be prevented.

It is unnecessary to describe at greater length the general state of disturbance and the half-convulsive attitudes into which the body is thrown by the pressure of mental emotions. One group of special importance must, however, be singled out from the multitude. Where the mental agitation contains likewise a motive to a particular action, gestures make their appearance which either copy that action in miniature or exhibit it in its first stage—*e.g.*, the gestures of anger when its object is in sight, or at least known. On the other hand, where the mind is helplessly tossed to and fro in a sea of pain or pleasure, the internal agitation finds vent chiefly in the most various changes of the breathing, or rather limits itself to this mode of expression, which is never wholly absent in the already-mentioned contortions. In joy, in grief, in surprize, respiration becomes unequal, accelerated, and deep, or rapid and short, or remittent, irregular, more like a sigh; with emotion is associated the tremulous movement that takes the place of the quiet, uniform activity of the respiratory muscles and precedes an outburst of sobbing; anger and rage for a moment keeps back the deep-drawn breath, that, after the fashion of all assailants, it may meet its object with firm-braced chest; the fury that has no object on which to expend itself begins to snort, intentionally executing and exaggerating respiratory movements that at other times go on instinctively and imperceptibly; finally, in laughter, delight in a harmlessly absurd incongruity breaks out in spasmodic working of the muscles of respiration. All these convulsive movements have the conspicuous peculiarity that nothing is effected by means of them; with air for their material and no aim at any product whatever any more than a direction toward any definite end, they are the purest expression of mere excitement, pleasurable or painful. Even as such they would afford the onlooker a vivid and faithful picture of the internal state; but Nature has attached the vibrating bands of the vocal ligaments to the system of the respiratory organs, and thus gives an opportunity to the faintest ingredients of this aimless disturbance to embody themselves in the audible tones of the voice, and to make themselves heard at a distance in the outer world. So in the animal kingdom we have the sound of pain and the sound of joy—infinitely poorer in definite indication of objects and actions than the rudest gesture, in expression of the hidden emotion itself incomparably richer than any other means which living races could have chosen for mutual communication. For as a photographic likeness is the exact reproduction of the form, so is the voice in its pitch, its peculiar timber, and the degree of steadiness, strain and loudness the direct audible likeness of the innumerable minute and finely knitted impressions produced by the emotion of the mind on the mobile masses of the body.

The view has been held that speech was an invention, in such a sense that out of several means of communication men deliberately chose this; but there certainly is no fear of its being revived in these days, and the foregoing remarks show how, on the contrary, by a naturally predetermined physiological necessity, the soul is compelled to express in tones at least the general character of its inner states. But we are still a long way distant from human language, and modern theorists who content themselves with admiring the organic unity and connection of the thought-forming fantasy and the sound-forming voice, overlook a great number of intermediate links, some of which it is quite requisite to mention.

Nature has bestowed voice on many races of animals; many develop it into song, none into speech. The question arises, what is the cause of this? Is it that the animals are without any matter which they have the desire to express, or that they are prevented from doing so by some physical obstacle? However the case may stand with the content of animal consciousness, I can not be one of those who answer the latter question in the negative, for I am convinced that defects of organization would in any case prevent the development of the animal voice into speech, and that, on the other hand, man's superiority rests partly on the better organization peculiar to him. The anatomical investigation of the vocal organs which formerly led Rudolphi to make the assertion that the absence of speech in apes was at all events not determined by any deficiency in their organs, can at most prove that all the conditions of vocalization are present; and the most ordinary experience makes it needless to prove this. But speech develops itself out of voice through the articulation of sounds; and in the animal kingdom we find this either not at all or only in the most fragmentary form.

STUDIES IN PROSE

Taking as a basis of comparison the human system of vowel and consonant sounds, we may note as a remarkable fact, that while some birds can imitate our words, even this mechanical capability has never been observed in any mammal. And yet the formation of the cavity of the mouth, the teeth, the tongue, the palate, in this class of animals far more resembles the human than that of any bird. It may further be added that among the mammalia different particular consonants and vowels are actually to be met with divided among different species, tho in the same species they are never united into a compound speech sound. The dog says r and guttural ch very distinctly; the cat is acquainted with f; cows and sheep with nasal n, and we can hardly doubt that most of the fixt positions of the mouth on which our articulate sounds depend, would be mechanically possible to animals if only there were for their muscles an impulse to produce them, and for their fantasy an impulse to combine them together. But even the ape, with its propensity to mimicry, remains dumb; the dog, attentive as he is to the purport of our words, makes not the slightest attempt at speech; only birds repeat sounds made in their hearing, but by nature they, too, keep to the inarticulate tones and melodies of their kind. Now wherein lies the obstacle? In my opinion, in these two things: First, defective sense of hearing; and second, want of an organically constituted harmony between ideas of sound and the muscular movements that are requisite for the production of sounds.

Even the highest achievement of animals in the direction of voice-development, the song of birds, is remarkable for a total want of harmonious tone relations. The melody advances in the most irregular fashion; sometimes lingering on one note with all possible purity and with bewitching quality of voice; sometimes running through a series of sounds, in each of which an indefinite number of rapid transitions from one pitch to another are combined into a kind of chaotic noise; sometimes, finally, continuing through quarter tones or quite inharmonious intervals. There is no reason to suppose that the sequence of two pure tones forming a concord is impossible for birds, for they do occasionally make it; there is rather, evidently, an absence of any sensuous motive for preferring this sequence to any other. I am therefore of opinion that birds' ear and fantasy lack susceptibility for harmonic intervals, and that the scale seems to them only more or less in the matter of pitch, while the qualitative relations through which to us two tones at a wider interval in the scale may be more nearly related than two close together, are lost upon them. This defect would not be a decisive obstacle to speech but for its association with another which we also meet with in the voices of all animals. All are aware of the difficulty there is in expressing their sounds by a written notation, altho in the growling or snarl of dogs, when we think of it as divided into infinitesimal intervals of time, we have almost every one of these intervals filled with a particular vowel or consonant, yet the animals hardly ever keep their mouth for a measurable time in one position, and every definite sound has no sooner been uttered than it passes into another. While, then, the voices of dogs or oxen sound to a great distance, they never emit one unequivocal vowel, but from moment to moment hover between one and another. Here, too, I can not think that there is any muscular incapability to prevent the retention of the pure sound; rather I believe that to the ear of animals the distinctions of articulate speech-sounds, tho not incapable of being perceived, have no such emphatic esthetic value as to lead to any importance being attached to them. In this connection I must introduce a general remark in regard to the sound-material of speech, which forms a continuation of the reflections already made on the peculiar character of human sentience.

Were we to try to put into character all the vowel sounds that have been emitted by individuals or by nations, we should require a countless multitude of signs; but it is at once apparent to our natural feeling that this multitude of different sounds have not all a uniform value. On the contrary, there stands out from among them a very small group as pure primitive vowels, distinguished not only by being recognized as simple elements in our now fixt written language, but by having in themselves an obviously distinct character and a special value. Between these fixt points, *a, e, i, o, u,* we insert all other vowel sounds as deviations, approximations, obscurations, and mixtures, just as we reduce the endless variety of tints to a small group of simple primary colors. Thus to our ear the innumerable vowel sounds are by no means a vague, confused host, that we might increase by the addition of new vowels at any moment when we either gave ourselves trouble to put our mouth into an unusual attitude, or chose to suppose that our vocal organs were differently constituted. The group is a closed one in spite of the endless number it contains, for there are fixt points between which all other conceivable modifications must take their place. The vowels then stand before our imagination as a system, a regular series of intrinsic value, so that our voice in pronouncing them does not emit arbitrary sounds, but subjects itself to the inherent necessity and regularity of a scale which would be such even if no one had ever embodied its parts in speech. In spite of the obscurity still hanging over the physical conditions under which the several vowels arise, the supposition is probable that in the five simple ones the manifold reverberation of the sound-waves of the voice within the cavity of the mouth produce a particularly simple, regular, and symmetrical development and intersection of rarefaction and condensation, so that the total movement of the particles of air, could it be made visible, would form for each of these vowels a figure whose formula could easily be stated. Hence it may arise that these sounds alone appear to us pure, genuine, normal, and simple, and that our ears seek to derive all others from them as compound or mixed. Now this susceptibility for such an objective truth in sounds is what I would assign to the human sense of hearing in contrast to the animal; and the more delicate this power of discrimination the more will sentience strive to reproduce these sounds, through the voice as their productive organ, and to reduce and articulate the chaotic sum of possible sounds into these sharply separated elements.

It would be more difficult to prove the same in regard to the consonants; but a glance at their application in languages shows with what delicacy their mutual affinity is felt, and I think that one would perceive this affinity immediately from their sound, even were one not clear as to the analogy between their modes of origination. Palatals are by every one, apart from any theory, discriminated from others as a connected group of sounds passing into one another. Now, I do not believe that any speech could be formed for the expression of thought were all this otherwise; did not the whole material of sound stand before us as an objective system of tones, each several member sharply discriminated from the others and yet allied with many by natural affinities, each one pure and distinct, yet capable of grouping around itself a multitude of proximate modifications. From this point of view it is intelligible that human speech has not adopted a considerable number of sounds which we can unquestionably make, but which are too indistinct in their relations of affinity with others to be utilizable material; it is further not probable that speech in the earliest stage of its growth was content with the three vowels, *a*, *i*, *u*, as the most sharply discriminated and those which alone are perfectly pure, and that not till later did it recognizes *e* and *o*, which, without deliberate attention, are never sustained pure, but pass into *i* and *u*. I do not mean that only those three have from the first actually been uttered; on the contrary, that strange phenomenon in speech-consciousness, of sounds and words being different in name from what they are as spoken, may have showed itself at an early period—curious conflict that it is between the conception of the sound as it by rights must be and the facility of uttering it. It seems to me natural, however, that in its first exercise this working fantasy should most readily exhibit its arbitrary legislation, or recognition of law, in the harshest and sharpest contrasts; a phonic system so weakened and moving by preference among such minute distinctions as, for instance, the English language, at present can belong only to a time that puts together breccias and conglomerates out of earlier original formations.

My original intention, therefore, was to show that by the human sense of hearing are discriminated distinctions in sounds which to that of animals are not indeed as zero, yet are not perceived in the full significance of their mutual relations. This by itself would explain the absence of spontaneous production of these sounds; but I added above the conjecture that, besides, the difficulty of producing them is increased by imperfection in the mechanics by which the voice is moved. The process by which all voluntary movements are executed is, as we have already shown, concealed from consciousness; the image of the new position to be effected, and the remembrance of the peculiar modifications of our general sense by which on former occasions its *execution* was accompanied, are the sole two points appearing in consciousness, to which the carrying out of the movement itself is subsequently attached by means of an unconscious and automatically working mechanism. In the case of speech, the auricular image of the sound to be produced takes the place of the ocular image of the movement to be performed. To the actual utterance of the sound it is now indispensable that along with this auricular image—which we must conceive both as a mere internal psychic state, but also as a slight stimulation of the auditory nerve thence proceeding—be associated by an organic arrangement the impulse to a distinct muscular movement, namely, to that complex movement by which all the organs concerned in the production of a sound are moved into the necessary relative situations. Where this organic provision is lacking, the conception of the sound may be present, but it will not be manifested in movements of the vocal organs. Now, I think that in general there is such an arrangement of the nerves in all animals endowed with voice; but in man alone probably is this organ so exquisitely developed that there is not only a power of discriminating between the most various sounds as to their pitch no less than as to their melodiousness and timber, but also a finely organized adaptation of the motor nerves to the reproduction of all these peculiarities. This is what might be called a corporeal organ of speech; for the body's contribution to the formation of speech can not extend certainly further than to placing at the soul's disposal this pliable medium of expression, and to inducing it to make use of the same by means of the already mentioned physiological impulse. Physiologists seem, in fact, to have been so fortunate as to discover the organ in one of the anterior convolutions of the cerebral lobes—injury in this spot being followed by aphasia, *i.e.*, want of power to make the desired speech-movements follow the conceptions of sounds.

When we compare the training of speech to deaf mutes with the training of parrots, we find that one and the same result is reached from two different starting points. The former are deficient in conceptions of sound, but their organs of speech are constituted like those of their speaking teacher. By means of their human capacity of attention they can therefore be brought by careful and laborious training not only to form a conception of the particular movement of these organs that corresponds to a seen character, but also to execute this movement and produce the required tone. Now, the feeling of movement experienced by the deaf mute during utterance forms for his memory in future the starting-point which his consciousness first repeats on meeting again with the character, and which then is followed with mechanical ease by the renewed execution of the movement. Of course the modulation of speech so acquired will never quite lose the harshness proceeding from the want of a perception of the produced result. The bird under training, on the other hand, has the conception of the sound, but externally his organs are so unlike those of his human teacher that his animal intelligence finds the chief difficulty in guessing how the latter produces the sound, and how he himself must manage his differently constructed vocal organs in order to produce the same. Obviously this can be done only if the bird's organization is such that the tone-conception, in so far as it is at the same time stimulation of the nervous tract, acts directly on the vocal nerves, and at once effects for the bird what he could not of himself bring about. To the human child only this mode of learning to speak is natural; it learns words not by watching the mouth, but through its vocal organs being directed by its conception of sound. Two things are remarkable: the extraordinary interest with which the child devotes himself to this working of his organs of motion, and at the same time the trouble which it costs him to become fully master of them. At a time when the motion of the other parts of the body is far behind the agility already attained by animals of the same age, there awakes—generally along with pantomimic movements—the effort to talk by means of the most marvelous curling of the lips, contortions of the mouth, and movements of the tongue; while usually the power of moving the palate and back parts of the cavity of the mouth is acquired later. By observing these phenomena one can obtain ocular evidence of the working of a physiological impulse evidently here impelling the inner states of the general sense into this particular form of expression. And the difficulty which, nevertheless, is met with in bringing these movements wholly under control in no wise tends to weaken our conviction of an organic foundation for them. Just as the eyes, whose whole structure undoubtedly is adapted for the regular uniting of the rays of light, do not perform this office immediately after birth—nay, are scarce capable of discerning a faint gleam of light—so probably the delicate perception of distinctness in tones and sounds is not from the first present in perfection, but is gradually developed out of an indefinite susceptibility to sound in general, in proportion as its delicacy increases, the instinctive working of its stimulations on the vocal organs also becomes more distinct.

I close these observations on the share of the body in the formation of speech with a summary glance over a field that the wider scope of these inquiries does not permit of my examining. That the bodily organization should have a share in the conditions of speech will not seem unnatural to those who bear in mind that we are here dealing not so much with an operation of the mental energy itself as with the manifestation of this operation in the form of a physical phenomenon. Here the mind is not at home, and it suffers no loss of dignity by having its medium of expression sound, and the power of using this medium conferred on it without any choice of its own by independent bodily impulses. In the further development of speech traces of this physiological influence may still be discerned in some of the phenomena. Not merely the general selection of the sounds utilized in the language of any particular people may proceed from minute peculiarities in the structure of its vocal organs, again in part perhaps dependent on climatic conditions (*e.g.*, we find widely diffused among the inhabitants of mountainous countries a preference for the harsh palatal sounds, and among dwellers in islands for dental consonants); but also the modifications of vowels and consonants in the inflexion and composition of words suggest the idea of their being, in part at least, the result of organic conditions. But the precise nature of these it would be very difficult to state. Already we tread on doubtful ground in asking whether the tendency to these alterations in sounds is acoustic or phonetic—I mean, whether they are made in order to offer the ear a euphonious balance in the distribution and succession of heavier and lighter sounds, in harmony especially with the accentuation, so that the complete word may float before the sense of hearing like a correctly drawn and proportioned figure; or whether it is mainly the convenience of the vocal organs (which do not slip with equal ease from every position into every other, and can not repeat every movement frequently in succession) that leads, above all things, to a construction of sounds that are easy of pronunciation. This last influence tells in the vulgar pronunciation of words correctly known; on the other hand, the explanation of the fact that in most languages the words borrowed from another, especially the proper names, are modified in accordance with native usage, is to be found not always in phonetic convenience, but frequently also in the need felt to convert the foreign into the familiar structure of sounds, as if that alone were normal and correct. Nay, a third cause—of grammatical character—may often concur—*e.g.*, a sequence of sounds that in compound words is avoided as disagreeable by modification of a primitive vowel occurs in close juxtaposition in the inflexion of a simple word, and here does not call forth the slightest effort at alteration. Neither the auricular image of it, then, is in itself displeasing, nor is the pronunciation difficult, but it is displeasing in comparison with the syntactic value of the one word, and pleasing in comparison with that of the other.

This last remark leads us to the point where, strictly speaking, human speech begins. From what has gone before, nothing more could be inferred than a tendency to a musical exercise of the voice that renounced the attempt to make use of differences of pitch, and employed instead varieties in sounds. Language begins with the meaning attached to these sounds, and the peculiar form of thought into which that meaning is thrown—a form which is either itself also exprest in sounds, or, remaining unexprest, makes the significant sound into a word capable of being syntactically combined with others.

Of these various elements, taking first into consideration the contained meaning, we know that nowadays it is handed on exclusively by transmission from one to another, and that our sentient fantasy is utterly incapable of divining from the sound of the words in a civilized language a meaning such as shall necessarily correspond to it. It is supposed that in the infancy of speech this was not so; that then each one, at least of the simple sense-perceptions that men first strove to communicate, had a sound answering to it, and that it is possible in root words to recognize the meaning attached by the still unsophisticated and fresh fantasy of man to each vowel and each consonant, and each simple combination of them. Perhaps it is the fault of our present artificiality that we have no longer any feeling of this, and that—to be candid—most roots seem to us to have come by their meaning quite as a matter of chance; at all events nothing is more precarious than any attempt now to prove the inherent necessity of the connection between the two. Two things we must, moreover, take into account. The physiological tendency with which we have become acquainted would in itself lead only to the expression of the particular kind and amount of mental stimulation produced in us by an impression from without, but it would throw no light on the nature of the cause of this impression. According to the varying degree of mental susceptibility, partly individual and permanent, partly belonging to the moment, the stimulation produced by the same irritant would prove very variable, and here one sound, there another, would with equal physiological necessity attach itself as a name to the same thing. Tolerably similar designations could be expected only for such objects or events as exert an influence powerful enough to compel similar stimulations in every frame of mind. But we allow that there is another tendency of the fantasy, whose office it is, abstracting from the nature of the passive subjective state, to present a copy of the objective character of the irritant whence the impression proceeds. To this tendency we must in great part attribute the development of language, which even in its beginnings was no mere collection of emotional utterances, but with genuinely human comprehensiveness of interest strove to communicate also the tranquil moods of mind and the passionless results of the train of thought. The result of this representative tendency would, however, be uniform and general only supposing our sentience found in the single sounds with which it had to work a decided similarity to perceptible qualities of things, and to the forms of events. A perfectly plain and directly intelligible system of symbols would then instruct every one to associate with a particular idea only one particular sound, with the sound only that idea. But clearly this is not the case, and can not be the case, because most objects of perception present a number of marks, and yet no rule determines in what order of sequence our attention is to combine these, or which it is to single out and make the basis of nomenclature. After all, then, only those words are directly intelligible which imitate an actual natural sound—a restricted and comparatively unimportant part of the stock of language.

Let us, then, be content to leave undecided the origin of the simplest words; there is still a rich field for a research confining itself to tracing the paths by which the fantasy of races, out of the few terms for sensibly perceived objects that doubtless formed the original amount of their store of words, has gradually acquired expressions for the endless variety of supersensible ideas and their subtle and complex relationships. We shall find, if we devote ourselves to this employment, that in the attempts to denote new objects or new results of reflection by judicious comparison with others already known or named, there is displayed, not only an exceedingly vigorous activity of the comparative imagination, but activity of a kind that enters essentially into the mental character of a nation and its mode of conception. The analogies, similes, and images which in our developed languages only poetry still employs, in order to replace the now ineffective diction of every-day life by expressions whose meaning, not yet worn threadbare, again brings freshly home to us the value of what they denote. All these means belong naturally to the youth of language, and the flowery speech of many tribes not cultivated by reflection resembles in this respect not a little the manner of expression common to its earliest stages. Many a word that now briefly and with clean-cut impress denotes an object indeed, but seems to tell nothing about its nature, contains in its original full form—which etymological research can sometimes trace—a significant attempt at a theory, at an explanation of the thing denoted. Of course, the strange error is not now to be justified of seeking to determine the nature of things from the meaning of their names, and of taking the notions deposited in these names by the word-forming fantasy of primitive times as a clue to guide us in attaining a knowledge of the things named. There is, however, a deep interest—and one not foreign to our subject—in observing what particular attribute of an object most strongly attracted that fantasy by its novelty or its importance, hence causing the name to be fixt with reference to it. We should frequently find how delicate was the comparative perception of these times of which no historic retrospect can now be distinct, with what susceptibility it often laid hold of the most general and not always the most obvious resemblances and connections of phenomena, and how even in languages of different types the similar comparisons implied in their terms for the same objects not seldom offer individual instances of a surprizing identity of procedure in the common human fantasy. But these fascinating researches, which become convincing and instructive only through the collection of a mass of details, lie outside the narrower path here prescribed to us. We can take up language again only after it has reached a stage of its growth at which the primitive meaning of these picturesque word formations has long since been forgotten. Most of the syllables that at first, through association with perceived phenomena, figuratively exprest the character of a notion, have passed into inflections, terminations, and prefixes, and serve only to indicate sharply, but with colorless abstraction, the formal setting that thought seeks to give to the content of the main constituent of the earlier compound.

STUDIES IN PROSE

In now entering on the consideration of this relation between speech and thought, we are about to encounter questions that in themselves are not very obscure and scarcely to be called equivocal, yet which, in consequence of the one-sidedness with which they were formerly discust, have given rise to much hot disputation. Whatever more strict sense we may give to the term thought, at any rate speech is not thought itself but its expression, and further, the expression, not of it alone, but also of every other movement of mind—of passion no less than of tranquil feeling. Now it is easy to see that speech may pass over much that thought, in order to be complete, must include; as in every-day conversation many connecting members are left to be understood by the listener, so even the typical forms of construction of a language may be an incomplete, but for all purposes sufficient, expression of the articulation of thought. It is then to make a needless demand to require that the verbal organization of discourse shall fully correspond to the logical organization of thought. On the other hand, the end of speech is not merely to be a brief communication of thoughts; in order to move the mind of another, to persuade, to set forth his own feeling with picturesque clearness, and to reproduce it in his hearer, to indicate his own conviction or uncertainty, to discriminate between the doubting query and the assertion, between the direct demand and the more modest wish, between indignant rejection of an idea and its mere denial—for all these purposes the speaker must be able to invest the content proper of his thought in manifold forms that add no material part to the logical structure of his sentence, yet throw over all its parts a peculiar coloring of merely psychological significance. Of course the sum of these secondary determinations might, if one cared to take the trouble, be also broken up into sentences of logical brevity, and in this form be added to the main affirmation; but it is certainly not the natural office of speech to say ineffectively and in a prolix manner what it can say shortly and emphatically. On the other hand, there can be added with equal facility those other qualifications which belong to the thought in its completeness, but are passed over; and to do this is of more use. For very often logic, altho all it has to do is to inquire what is the thought underlying any proposition, no matter how much of it is exprest, has allowed itself to be led by the incompleteness of the expression into needless and protracted questionings.

But one thing must be borne in mind: to whatever extent language is designed to include the subtlest movements of feeling, only such exhibitions come within the province of speech as are in some way exprest under the forms of thought. No more than the modula-

STUDIES IN PROSE

tion of the voice and the accompanying gesture does the mere sound of exclamation belong to language, even when its meaning is unequivocal; besides the articulation and significance of the sound, there must be further a peculiar form of intelligent conception that makes the sound a word, and gives it its syntactical value. In order to review these relationships, we must enter at some length into the peculiar nature of thought and the very close connection betwen it and language that has induced us to subject to a common examination these two characteristic elements of human culture.

On the former occasion I endeavored to illustrate a distinction which we have to make between the *thinking* that alone deserves that name *par excellence,* and the *train of ideas* produced by the universal laws of psychic mechanism in all animated beings in like manner, but with very different degrees of vivacity. In the latter our consciousness is mainly receptive and passive; it receives the various impressions that beset it from the environment with or without connection, with or without order, as chance brings them; further, it permits memory, according to the general rules of the association and recollection of ideas, to repeat the several impressions in the same combination, sometimes significant, sometimes meaningless, in which they were held in the original perception. It might seem that a long continuance of this train of ideas would gradually of itself eliminate the accidental character of its connection; for in the course of things unconnected details do indeed sometimes occur together, but not in constant conjunction. When, therefore, we survey a considerable tract of our experience, we find that the more numerous combinations of connected objects gain the preponderance over the more rarely repeated combinations of the phenomena brought together merely by chance. Thus are gradually formed fixt images of particular objects, which detach themselves as permanently coherent groups of attributes from other shifting perceptions; from the concatenation of events there arise distinct remembrances that lead us instinctively to expect from present circumstances those consequences which actually flow from them with natural consistency. But however sufficiently in this manner the thus improved train of ideas may qualify the soul of an animal for finding its place in the sphere of its experience and attending to the gratification of its appetites, there is yet an utter absence of one mental operation which, as we have found, forms part of human thought. We do not at first merely receptively and passively receive the partly correct, partly incorrect combinations of impressions presented by perception, and later the amended selection of these left behind by the self-correcting movement of the psychic mechanism. Our thought, with independent action, breaks up the accidental associations of ideas, and, instead of merely leaving intact those which are coherent, put them through a process of reproduction, after which they appear in forms that at the same time contain an indication of the reason why they are combined. Even animal consciousness is right as to the content of its thought when, with the image of a burden about to be laid on, it associates the anticipation of a painful pressure; the human judgment, *the burden is heavy,* adds nothing to this content, but, making the burden the subject out of which the pressure flows, it vindicates the combination of the two conceptions from the nature of their content, from the connection between cause and effect, and explains the merely actual combination of the two in consciousness by an objectively valid law, in virtue of which they cohere. It is needless to accumulate examples of this kind; if the mechanism of ideation provides not only for the bringing together of the content of consciousness, but also to a certain extent for the elimination of the essentially coherent from the accidentally combined, yet it is *thinking* alone that exercises on this content, that constant criticism by means of which our hypotheses in regard to the necessary connection of all things and events are worked up into a perception of the same, and the merely intuitive picture drawn by sentience and psychic mechanism, is quickened by a discernment of the internal bonds that hold together its several points.

This peculiar activity of thought comes to manifestation in the organization of language, and on the other hand is aided by the latter in its operations. To consider, first, the first part of this relationship, it is not necessary that each several operation of thought should have its own special expression; but language must separate from one another the simple elements of thought, by whose employment and combination all the more refined and elevated offices of thought are fulfilled, in forms that make such employment possible. It is not, it appears to me, fitting to begin the treatment of logic, as is usually done, with an investigation of the simplest form of combination in which thought unites heterogeneous mental elements. There is a still simpler and a prior task which it has perforce to fulfil; it has to give to every simple element, in order to make it capable of combination with others, a definite form through which, from a mere impression, the raw product of psychic stimulation, it is transformed into an organically utilizable thought-atom. The combinations into which thought strives to bring the manifold content are distinguished especially by the prominence in them of internal architectonic structure from the mere conglomeration which the psychic mechanism is adequate to effect. Stones can always be piled in a heap, whatever their form, if it does not matter how they are arranged; an edifice that is to be borne up and sustained by forces working in diverse directions can not be put together out of merely spherical constituent parts—for any design and plan the stones must be hewn into such shapes that they may mutually strengthen one another, and offer notched surfaces for adhesion and dovetailing. In like manner thought can not directly make use of sensations, feelings, moods, simple or complex images, as materials for its structure; each of these elements, which are primarily but states of stimulation, it must apprehend in a form that in the subsequent combination decides on the manner of its employment and the particular fashion in which it is grouped with others. Language exhibits this first operation of thought in the distinction of its parts of speech. Inasmuch as it apprehends a content substantively, it recognizes it as something independent, self-sufficing, capable of acting as the starting-point of a second and the point of destination of a third content; complete in itself and a self-sufficing whole, the substantive is the natural form in which the primitive language-builders express the notion of a *thing*, and which they therefore at first used to designate nothing that does not present itself to the eye of sense-perception as an independent object.

The content stamped with the adjective character is thereby declared to be not independent, to be something whose existence, definite quantity, form, and limitation come from another and a substantive content, on which it is of necessity in a perpetual state of dependence; and the sensible properties of things, as exhibited by these in a state of repose, are what first held fast in this form of adjectivity. To these elements language adds the third and indispensable one of the verb, in order to indicate the flux by which the course of events connects together these motionless images; this, too, is a form at first intended for the reflection of sensible changes, but soon employed also to express relationships between things in repose—from the movement of our comparative thought, by which alone we apprehend relationships, being interpreted as reciprocal movements of the subjects of the relationships.

It is enough to have spoken of these three forms which are indispensable to speech; let us leave to philology not only the question which of them is the more original, and prior to the others, but also the genetic history of other forms which, as prepositions and conjunctions, by the introduction of complex notions of relation, elaborate language into a perfectly pliable medium of expression for thought. Let us be content with clearly recognizing that those three forms present the minimum of organization and division of presented matter with which thought can attempt to begin its operations. Without them our train of ideas would be but a silent, our speaking but an audible, strain of music; ideas and tones might indeed refer to one another and reveal their affinities and antagonisms to feeling, but all the sharply discriminative arrangement would have disappeared that had been established by a definite form of inner connection. However full of meaning the music of a song may be, it is quite different in character from the words; no note in it is anything substantive waiting for an adjective attribute to be attached to it; none more than the rest expresses action proceeding from another as its living subject, and passing over to a third as its passive object. Never do two tones enter into one of those manifold articulate relations which language denotes by the cases of substantives, by the active and passive voices of verbs; the genitive that joins the possessor to the possession; the accusative that connects with the agent the result of his action, musical harmony has no means adequate to express. Now this is what we signalized above as the peculiar function through which the significant sound really becomes a word; for it is not made such by its significance; on the contrary, the interjections which most purely and directly express psychic excitement form an unorganized residue of the material of language. The sound becomes a word by means of the logical accessory thoughts displayed in the character of the parts of speech; they serve as uniting surfaces and joints for the various contents, which thus become capable of syntactic combination in the service of thought.

I do not think much of the objection to this view drawn from the fact that in many languages the distinction between the parts of speech is not embodied in special sound-forms answering severally to each. What is of consequence is not that the form of our thought should be reflected in that of the sound, but only that it should be present as an accompanying act of thought. Whether or not a language indicates its substantives by any external mark, its syntactically formless word is nevertheless made into a substantive by the mind of the speaker who utters it with the thought of the substantiality of its content. Thought is not so absolutely dependent on language that combinations of sounds are of necessity the medium through which it expresses its formal conception of the content of presentations. Had Nature imposed instead of speech some other mode of expression on the human mind, it would have endeavored to express through this other medium in equivalent forms the same distinctions which we have in language under the form of parts of speech; even had no means of expression been

STUDIES IN PROSE

at its disposal, it would none the less have continued inwardly to make the same distinctions, tho in this case much hindered by the absence of the reflex assistance that thought receives from its external medium of expression. The grammatical form of language may therefore lag behind its logical articulation; but where it does so the language is in a backward stage, and every language free alike from primitive crudeness and from the disintegration of decay will express the logical distinctions of its stock of words even in their audible sound-structure. To a far greater extent, indeed, the language-forming fantasy goes beyond the needs of thought, and produces a great number of grammatical forms and syntactical rules that with the progressive advance of reflection are gradually allowed to drop as superfluous. Thus substantives and verbs have gradually lost the wealth of inflections that distinguished them in the earlier stages of language, and thought has learned, by putting together many auxiliary words, to replace the delicate shades of expression which they embodied; on the other hand, the variety of genders in substantives and adjectives, and the obligation on the latter to conform to the former, are still retained in different languages to different extents—a luxury of speech this, and an ingenious one, which yet forms merely a superfluous esthetic appendage to the logically necessary systematization of thought.

Superfluous, that is, if we choose to look on language as exclusively a reproduction of the most general means of thought, through whose arbitrary application the knowledge of things is to be attained. But unquestionably from the first it was meant to be more; a great part of the work that had to be done it has already done for consciousness. Every object of eternal perception, every event, every extended figure pictured by us in imagination, every relationship between several things, may be approached on different sides by our reflective attention. Almost every content, therefore, admits of more than one notion being formed of it, according as we begin our construction with this or that constituent or point of relation, and add the others in this or that order of succession. The names of objects in a language of long standing are sufficiently set free from remembrances of their earlier meaning, the forms of construction by which relationships are indicated have become sufficiently detached, to leave freer scope to the imagination in this affair of individual fancy; former generations must in this respect have felt themselves under greater restraint. From the origin of their words being still in remembrance, and the mode of their combination being under stricter regulation, they must have been surrounded as with an atmosphere of common, national thought, which had already fixt the standard of conception in regard to innumerable objects and relations of objects, and to continue to think in the spirit of this seemed naturally incumbent on the individual. This is the somewhat dubious gift of a developed language that invents and thinks for us. If, however, we consider the inestimable advantage accruing to each individual from the inexhaustible, boundless riches of the world of thought thrown open to him, which he would be wholly unable to create for himself by his own powers, we lose sight of the slight disadvantage of his being thus trained to certain one-sided modes of conception. At any rate, the effort to order one's own thoughts with unrestrained individual freedom can be made only when when it has a point of departure in this national treasure of wisdom handed down in the language, and can thence draw strength for progress. Besides, in course of time a change takes place in this relation between language and thought. The more men advance from simple conditions of life, in which the poetic and genial phase of social relationships prevails for good and for ill, to division of labor—set about reflecting on and examining the nature of things, and begin to speak more of business than of feelings—the more, in a word, the working prose of life becomes developed, so much the more does language drop the crude prejudgments concerning things which it originally contained. By the obliteration of their etymology its words become mere denotations by means of sounds; the pleasure in sound and its harmonic varieties dies away; old time-honored forms of construction perish in consequence of the practical need of terse and accurate modes of stating new relationships. Hence at last we find particular departments—as that of mathematics—advancing almost to independence of words, and avoiding the prolixity of speech by a mere sequence of sound-symbols, whose visible connection as written characters is often exprest merely by pauses and accentuations in speech. Hence, in general, in the course of a vigorous development, much outward beauty is lost, and those nations do not usually advance on this path which continue with much display of sonorous euphony to say little in many words.

In a survey of the historical development of nations, these relations, to which it is here sufficient to refer, would naturally receive fuller consideration. On the other hand, a more general inquiry to which we have here to devote ourselves, links itself on to these remarks on the reaction of language on the development of ideas. As speech has been called *thinking aloud,* so the converse proposition—that *thought is silent speech*—has not failed to make its appearance. None of the points connected with this subject has been the cause of more disagreement than this one.

STUDIES IN PROSE

On the one side, the capacity of speech is looked on as constituting the decisive superiority of human nature, and as alone enabling it to develop veritable thought out of the merely mechanical train of ideas; on the other, tho the advantages of speech are not denied, not only is thought held to be independent of it, but it sometimes seems doubtful whether they are not overweighed by the disadvantages entailed by the habit of mentally clothing all thoughts in words.

In this respect attention has often been called to the fact that, unknown to ourselves, a strange superstition grows up within us: How apt are we to fancy that an object whose properties we have examined thoroughly, and of which we have formed a complete image, is yet not fully known to us so long as we are ignorant of its name. The sound of the name seems suddenly to dispel this degree of obscurity, tho it adds nothing to the content—does not even always bring the light implied in indicating the particular place belonging to the object in a series, or within the sphere of some wider notion. Young botanists delight in learning the Latin names of wayside flowers, and go contented on their way only to be presently disturbed by a mountain that, strange to say, has no name, and so has properly speaking no right to be there. Now, what do they miss in the one case? What did they gain in the other? I can not look on this fancy as so insignificant as it appears—nay, I see in it a counterpart or continuation of the genuinely human mode of conception on which I dwelt in discussing sentience. We are not satisfied with the perception of an object; its existence becomes legitimate only when it forms part of a regular system of things that has its own significance quite apart from our perception. Now, if we can not actually fix the place occupied by a product of Nature in the universe, the name, at all events, allays our disquietude; it at least bears evidence that the attention of many others had already been directed to the object at which we are now looking; it assures us that the general mind has at least been engaged in assigning to this object its special place in the connection of a greater whole. On this account it is that a name given arbitrarily by ourselves is no name; it is not enough that a thing is called somehow by us; we must have its real name; the name must be evidence of its having been received into the world of the universally known and recognized, and thus confront individual caprice as the peculiar and abiding determination of the thing. How little is this attended to by those who allow themselves to be led by the trifling peculiarities of their subjective line of thought, by the whims of their imagination, eager for new and capricious paths, to clothe old thoughts in an unusual phraseology, to overturn the established nomenclature of the sciences, and to perform the marvelous feat of calling all things by other than their names! Only the first discoverer of an object, or the first inventor of a scientifically efficient abstraction, is entitled to bestow the name under which he takes possession for science of this newly won point.

More serious is the other complaint, that during the long use of speech a multitude of modes of expression are accumulated, which, by means of the syntactic pliability of language, can be very conveniently combined together, but with which thought can not keep pace. Much can be done with words, and as what is evidently nonsense must admit of being, grammatically and syntactically, quite correctly and elegantly exprest, even that it may be examined and denied; still more, by the readiness with which a grammatically faultless form can be assumed, half-true, confused, distorted statements may be made to deceive by an appearance of perfect correctness. These processes can be most clearly traced in the combinations of mathematical symbolic language. Many particular groups of signs bearing on one another, at first devised for a special case to express a relation there comprehensible, may afterward be made to undergo a series of changes or of applications that for the moment have no assignable meaning, may frequently receive none even when we continue to calculate with them, yet sometimes lead to the discovery of new and veritable relations, whose meaning we only afterward begin to understand. The pliability of language very rarely indeed leads to such favorable results; for the most part, it only suggests modes of conception that depart further and further from the truth. We must be content to adduce a single but comprehensive example of this very fruitful source of error. The substantive form belongs originally only to things, the adjective form to qualities, the verb form to events. But, of course, language could not in its judgments always begin with the thing, and annex qualities and action to this as the subject; it had to make the qualities in themselves and action in itself also matter of its reflection. Hence it severed their connection with things, and gave *them* a substantive form, either by adding a peculiar termination to express this new character, or by transforming the infinitive of the verb or the neuter of the adjective into a consistent, complete, and independent whole by means of a prefixt article. When we survey the still continued controversies of scientific men, who are mainly occupied with general notions, and can not protect themselves from error by the constant check of regulative perception of some sort, we can not but acknowledge that nothing is more fatal than this one case of the pliability of language. Almost invariably we find a tendency to make the newly acquired syntactic dignity of words convertible with a new metaphysical dignity acquired by their matter. Thus, we have almost ceased to speak of beautiful objects—*i.e.*, we forget that what we call *beautiful* is originally a mere adjective determination not existing apart from a subject; we speak now of *the beautiful*, or at the best of *beauty*, and our esthetic thinkers are quite convinced that what can exist only as an attribute is correctly apprehended only when it has unnaturally been apprehended as something substantive which is everywhere identical. Need we recall the host of similar instances—*the infinite, the evil* —or speak of the mischief wrought in ethical inquiries by the habit of speaking, not of the freely willing mind, but of *freedom;* as if it were a power acting independently, whose energy and achievements could be judged without reference to the nature of the mind to which it pertains?

In all these cases languages creates for us a mythology, from which, of course, in the use of language we can never wholly set ourselves free without becoming pedantically precise, but against the influence of which on the molding of our thoughts we ought to be carefully on our guard. Logic does not always assist us in this direction, nay, sometimes in its methods makes pernicious concessions to this false tendency arising from the use of language. It requires that a term to be defined shall be subordinated under a higher general notion (which, of course, is always put into substantive form), a special mark being added. In this way adjectival and verbal contents under the process of definition lose their natural form and position, which they would retain if the same plan were pursued as in plain people's awkward but more correct attempts at definition. It may be a matter of comparative indifference whether one says that, *Disease is any departure of the body from its normal state,* or prefers to say that, *A living body is diseased when it is not in this normal state;* but the latter definition, in which what can not exist save as the state quality of something else appears as an adjective, and is distinctly annexed to the subject in which alone it has its being, is formally the more correct and the more suitable. Tho we may affirm that, *Elasticity is that property of bodies by which they return to their original form,* the proposition, *A body is elastic when it does this,* is unquestionably to be preferred; for the first form plainly contains the germ of a metaphysically false conception sure to be developed out of such use of terms, namely, the conception of a property, which is nothing else than the denotation of an effect, as the efficient cause or productive means of that effect. Mathematics and Physics, to which almost all that still remains of true and fruitful logic has betaken itself, have adopted this hypothetical form of definition wherever definition is required by the nature of the subject.

But language does not exist solely to minister to thought, and to our poetically living and sympathetic apprehension of the world and its events that substantializing of dependent conceptions is no less indispensable than it is dangerous for thought. The same holds true of another drawback of language which is but rarely felt, yet when it is plainly perceived, is seen to be of some magnitude. Seeing that in speech the elements of thought are only successively presented, even in the most natural style of expression it is impossible always to avoid an order of words occurring that does not answer to the combination of the ideas denoted by them; but in a cultured style, with its tendency to intertwine much that in simpler speech is exprest in detached coordinate clauses, there is often a most striking perversion of the order apparently required by the general purport of the context. Undoubtedly an awkward use of these liberties is felt as cumbrous obscurity; but how much can be tolerated in this respect by our conceptive and constructive imagination is shown most plainly by the collocation of words in Latin poetry. Even where they divide closely coherent and separately unintelligible parts of the discourse, we yet can often hit upon a manner of reading and accenting such as even in this situation enables us to discern their connection. In general, however, it seems to me a mistake to look upon that which most closely conforms to logical order as the best arrangement of words. On the contrary, one of the ends of language is to supply the place of perception. Now, as here, it very frequently happens that the unimportant comprehensive background or some striking detail first shows itself, and not till afterward the more important event, as the obvious effect comes before the hidden cause, or passivity on the one side before compensating activity on the other: so that discourse will be most distinct in which the several points of relation are marshaled in an order that brings them vividly before the reproductive imagination, no matter whether or not this corresponds to the logical order of the relations involved. For as even in perception our judgment in regard to this inherent connection is little affected by the order of succession in which objects happen to present themselves, so by thought we can very easily add to the given concrete image of an event those inherent relations by which it becomes intelligible; whereas the imagination has a highly difficult task when it is called on to represent successively certain relations at the bidding of the preceding words, before it knows the concrete concluding points toward which the thought is tending.

But if the deviation of spoken words from

the logical order of thought creates no serious difficulties, perhaps a more important hindrance is involved in the amount of time which words occupy. Not merely in communication, it may be said, does speech mean the extension of an opinion to be exprest, of a brief sum of meaning, into a long discourse; but, further, the habit of making use of its converts' inward reflection into silence discourse, and thus exerts a retarding influence. Thinking, of course, itself requires some time in order to perform its task of putting a variety of elements into relation; but the constant recollection of words needlessly protracts this time by its dependence on bodily conditions from which thinking could have kept itself free.

Many facts confirm this assertion. In trying to recall a melody, one finds oneself bound to a certain time; one can not imagine a series of tones gone through in less time than it would take to sing it—well or ill. For we involuntarily accompany the auricular images of tone with slight incipient movements of the vocal organs, and we can not make the former succeed each other more rapidly than the latter can follow upon one another. The musical expert may succeed in warding off this habit of retardation, and putting himself into the position purely of a listener with regard to the tone-images that revive in his memory; but even he will distinctly recall no greater number of these tone-images in the unit of time than the physiologically limited capacity of his auditory nerve would have allowed of his actually hearing within the same unit of time. We find the same thing in the recollection of words; the many trifling difficulties caused to a speaker by the alternation of vowels and consonants retard the succession in the word-images even in the mere representation of discourse. Not for all to the same extent, however; for the facility of muscular movement or of the varying impulses to it in different persons. It is found frequently, tho not without exception, that the propensity to rapid speech is inversely proportional to the length of the body. Very short people, just as from the shortness of their legs their pace is more swift and in general their heart-beat more frequent, have a natural tendency to speak quickly, and this whether they are also loquacious or whether they are taciturn, and only say rapidly the little they have to say. Tall persons will in general be found to speak slowly and phlegmatically; the rate of their discourse corresponds to their longer stride and greater slowness of heart-beat; for the rest, sometimes the stream of their discourse flows without interruption; sometimes they prefer to be silent on most subjects. It is long since these observations have become the property of the imitative imagination that moves in living human knowledge; with the aid of some exaggeration it has created out of small stature, with its sanguine, lively temperament, a familiar comic type, in which are embodied a ready wit, a disposition to become eager about petty ends, and a tendency to rashness of all sorts; whereas the tall, phlegmatic form—by dint of the same exaggeration a no less favorite character—has been taken by it for the expression of circumstantial thoroughness and tardiness in ever respect.

It is needless to inquire further into the accuracy of these trifling observations; even were they perfectly trustworthy, they would merely prove that our course of thought can not, so long as we convert its content into inward speech, exceed a moderate limit of velocity. But when we note the conscious impatience with which our thought often would fain hurry on, while yet it is compelled to linger over a simple idea till the compound term for it has been audibly recalled to mind, we are enabled by this further observation ourselves to reduce within its true dimensions the disadvantage supposed to proceed from our being habituated to language. For here we have evidence that this retarding recollection of words is not absolutely compulsory on our course of thought, which really outruns it, and that with us, as in the psychic life of the animals destitute of speech, a small space of time actually contains a great multitude of ideas in the regular coexistence and the methodical sequence in virtue of which they become the motive of a present purposive action. But could this movement of wordless ideation by itself accomplish all that is really achieved, however leisurely, by the course of our thoughts when shackled by a persistent remembrance of words?

This question, we believe, must be answered in the negative—those views be rejected in which, under the influence of an enthusiasm for the ineffable, language is regarded as a source of detriment to a coveted higher knowledge. All that thought must of necessity, nay does, possess together in one indivisible moment, language breaks up into a successive plurality, developing discursive thought out of the direct intuition of our representative faculty. Thought running backward and forward moves between the sundered elements of its content, which the obstinate temporal course of this silent speech never allows of its uniting. That relative thinking to which we have already ascribed the dignity of being the germ of all higher intellectual development, we here find censured as the meager form in which habituation to language permits of our performing high functions only inadequately. For does not all this putting in relation defeat its own end? Had our imagination not already under the guidance of slowly unfolding discourse divided the points that ought to be united, why should it require afterward laboriously to bring the scattered elements into relation? This were in vain, if in our representative activity we have forgotten the first point of relation by the time we have come to the second; superfluous, if it is possible for us simultaneously to grasp the two, and also their relation, at the same undivided moment.

In the first place, we must modify these accusations, for they touch not language alone, but even thought itself—nay, they touch our whole existence. Not only do we think discursively, but we also live so; not only do we elaborate perceptions in this fashion, but they present themselves in no other. At no moment are we both what we were and what we shall be; and even of what we are, we are at any one moment conscious to but a small extent. Objects present themselves alike fragmentarily to us; we do not feel the pulsation that is the inmost life of things going directly through our heart; the creative force that stirs in them, and the idea that binds their successive states into a whole, all this we must perforce seek to divine by means of the gradual combination of particular experiences; what in itself may be one, can not but be to us an extended network of relations between many things. If we desire, instead of this separation, that silent insight into things, not intuition of them, which forms our conception of the omniscient, toilless knowledge of God, we must be convinced that isolated moments of approach to such a state are granted to us, but that our incapacity to combine them into the permanent clearness of a thought without distinctions is the fault, not of language, but of our whole mental constitution. When we have listened to a poem recited, to a melody sung, and forget the words and the tones, while yet all that was in them lives on in an abiding mood of our soul; when, after long deliberation and weighing of *pros* and *cons,* we have at length come to a resolution, and in the purpose that now animates us feel combined and still efficient the impulses that before were severally weighed by our thought; when we first send our glance over the scattered details of a landscape, and then, after the definite outlines have long disappeared from our memory, still preserve an indelible total impression; we actually succeed in making that combination and fusion of myriads of details into the whole of a supersensible intuition, which we but reluctantly again analyze into its constituent parts in order to communicate it to others.

In all these cases we became something; the manifold did not remain outside of us, but the whole of its significant internal connection was repeated in a new state within ourselves with such perfection we could fancy we had transformed ourselves into the spirit of the phenomena that we admired. But only the Infinite Being that itself *is* all that it makes the object of its thought, could in this way enter into the being of all things, and, while entering into it, dispense with all the divining inquiry beginning from the outside. The finite mind has no alternative but to comprehend the nature of things by means of analogies with its own. For it volition is not equivalent to accomplishment, thinking to existence; for it the active and passive elements are separated from each other as diverse points, and it can apprehend the unity of what here is, and is done only as the transference of an action from one thing to another; it does not discern clearly how the manifoldness of successive phenomena is identical with the unity of being, and is forced to divide them as predicates from their subject, to which they are attached only by the thread of a relation; finally, for it, ends are not spontaneously achieved, by the one life of the idea, that is all in all, is converted into the cooperation of many means exhibiting themselves as independent of each other. All these analogies, these notions of things and property, of force and effect, of being and phenomenon, and all the forms of relation into which these *membra disjecta* are combined, must be employed by the human mind to gain a knowledge of things. And so indispensable to it is this putting into relation that even in any moment of exaltation in which we actually find and enter into a higher unity, we feel restless and uneasy till we have exprest its content in some form of the combination of the manifold in which it may be definitely fixt and again participated in by us in the movement hither and thither of thought. In each poetic imagination, before it has done its work, lies this mystic unity, and in doing it each seeks to escape from this; the best that we could ourselves be would not content us, because we can not be it otherwise than by spreading out its formless depth into the surface of a completely related phenomenon.

Language in all its operations is but the reproduction, not the cause, of this tendency of our mind. But, after having at such length stood on the defensive, I can more briefly add the positive assertion that even this form of thinking, the only one possest by us finite beings, would actually remain very imperfect, without this reproduction in language. Language, of course, does not impart to the mind the elements of thinking; but it indispensable when the mind has to combine these elements into the spacious fabric of its culture. As we always experience a refreshing effect from sense-intuition, and are not convinced of the success of any labor till we have before us some palpable result, so must the auricular images of names and the combinations of sounds that constitute grammatical and syntactical forms of speech, present to us in a fixt, sensible form, the former the multiplicity of things, the latter the systematic plurality of their possible relations. There can be no clearness of thought where the many presentations and groups of presentations that in mutual relation are to form a thought simultaneously occupy our consciousness without names, and only in their original character of affections of the soul; even tho thus they may be not a mere heterogeneous assemblage, but already held together by relations corresponding to those subsequently to be formulated, yet consciousness is not aware of this internal organization. It becomes to us real and true when in the task of statement we first bring one presentation into prominence, and then, guided by the syntactical form which we have given to its name, go beyond it in a definite direction, and rejecting on the way many others, succeed at last in putting into special connection with it the particular second presentation indicated by that direction. No thought is clear and distinct until it has undergone this process of analysis and recombination, and the simplest self-scrutiny may teach any one how, in proportion as the plastic form of the idea comes out into relief, the obscurities disappear that clove to it in its earlier unexprest stage. As a work of art can not be a full harmonious truth until it has been completed in marble or bronze, and as a conception in the artist's imagination is but a disjointed and fragmentary beauty, so for mankind language is the universal plastic material in which alone they elaborate their surging ideas into thought.

I have dwelt at special length on this point of view, which has a close affinity with that which throughout forms the fundamental thought of these inquiries, in the conviction that what we may take to be the highest content of the universe is to be conceived by us only as realized by a regular mechanism. I return but for a moment to the first form in which language exhibited itself to us. Originally designed as a medium of communication, it expanded unawares to us into an independent organism, over the development of which we have no control, and to whose inherent nature we must accommodate ourselves. Now, how much language even in this its primary function—*i.e.*, how much the possibility of conversation—contributes to high human development, needs no more than to be mentioned. It is an indispensable instrument not only of the first training, whose absolute necessity we shall subsequently feel, but also of the further cultivation of the already vitally stirring mind. A course of thought solitarily pursued by the individual, the direction of which only new external perceptions would alter, meets with salutary interruptions from the questions and answers of another; one-sided associations expand under the influence of a foreign world of thought

STUDIES IN PROSE

and feeling, which brings alike new intuitions and new points for the contemplation of those common to both. But why refer here in general to that to which our attention must subsequently be specially directed? Let us merely add that language renders similar services to the thought even of the individual when alone. By the sound of names, by their metrical rhythm in combination, are suggested to him attendant ideas and feelings, as well as remembrances of what is not present that would not in such abundance and distinctness accompany the dumb course of thoughts without words. As rime sometimes unexpectedly suggests to the poet a graceful conceit, so words in general, by means of the manifold associations cleaving to their meaning—so frequently figurative—guide our imagination along many paths that otherwise would be closed to it, that lead not always to the right goal, it is true—nay, often to a wilderness—but always disclose to us a rich field in which we can pick out the fruits that suit us.

How to Develop
Self-Confidence
in Speech and Manner

By GRENVILLE KLEISER

Author of "How to Speak in Public"; "How to Develop Power and Personality in Speaking," etc.

The purpose of this book is to inspire in men lofty ideals. It is particularly for those who daily defraud themselves because of doubt, fearthought, and foolish timidity.

Thousands of persons are held in physical and mental bondage, owing to lack of self-confidence. Distrusting themselves, they live a life of limited effort, and at last pass on without having realized more than a small part of their rich possessions. It is believed that this book will be of substantial service to those who wish to rise above mediocrity, and who feel within them something of their divine inheritance. It is commended with confidence to every ambitious man.

CONTENTS

Preliminary Steps—Building the Will—The Cure of Self-Consciousness—The Power of Right Thinking—Sources of Inspiration—Concentration—Physical Basis—Finding Yourself—General Habits—The Man and the Manner—The Discouraged Man—Daily Steps in Self-Culture—Imagination and Initiative—Positive and Negative Thought—The Speaking Voice—Confidence in Business—Confidence in Society—Confidence in Public Speaking—Toward the Heights—Memory Passages that Build Confidence.

12mo, Cloth. Write for Prices.

FUNK & WAGNALLS COMPANY, Publishers
NEW YORK AND LONDON

SPEECHES
OF
WILLIAM JENNINGS BRYAN

All who are called upon to speak from platform or pulpit can gain much from a study of William J. Bryan's methods.

This man probably has spoken to more people than any other man who ever lived. And—

His eloquence belongs to our own time—is a product of this day and generation—is the kind of speech used *effectively* before your fellow men TO-DAY.

Now for the *first* time his principal speeches have been printed in *two permanent volumes*, personally revised and arranged by the orator. Mrs. (Mary Baird) Bryan has added a biographical introduction, which we supplement with portrait illustrations showing Mr. Bryan at various ages.

Besides many famous political speeches, the two volumes contain these oratorical gems:—

"Patriotism," in London on Thanksgiving Day, "Man," "Radicalism and Conservatism," "The White Man's Burden," "Missions," "At the Peace Congress," "The Value of an Ideal," "Faith," "The Prince of Peace," "The Price of a Soul," "Character," "Presenting a Copy of Gray's Elegy," "To His Neighbors," "Memorial Day at Arlington," "At His Reception in Lincoln," "Commerce," "The Conservation of Natural Resources," "Lincoln as an Orator," "Dreamers."

"Not a few judges pronounce Mr. Bryan the greatest living orator in the English language."—*Toronto Globe.*

"Mrs. Bryan deserves great credit for her critical appreciation of her husband's work and place in the world."—*N. Y. Press.*

*Two volumes, bound in Cloth or Half Leather.
Write for Prices.*

FUNK & WAGNALLS COMPANY, Publishers
NEW YORK AND LONDON